THE HOUR WE LEAST EXPECTED

Please return to
Connie Nelson

The Hour We Least Expected

An Insightful Re-Examination of the Most Important and Unexpected Hour in Human History

Steve Essary Jr.
&
Aaron Essary

THE HOUR WE LEAST EXPECTED

ISBN-10: 0-615-45846-7
ISBN-13: 978-0-615-45846-5

Unless otherwise indicated, all scriptures quoted are taken from the New King James Version.

Other scripture quotations are taken from one of the following, as indicated in the text:

Printed in the United States of America

www.thehourweleastexpected.com

Steve's Dedications

I would like to thank my ex-wife, Kelly, for enduring, with me, many years of life changing chaos and for having and helping me to raise our wonderful kids.

I would like to dedicate this book to my wonderful children; Logan and Jackson, that they may always know the true love of God and never be held back by imaginary rules.

Aaron's Dedications

I would like to thank my wife, Jerrie Rose, for all of the love and patience ☺ you have shown me over the course of our lives together.

I would like to dedicate this book to my children. To my sons, Aaron and Benjamin; may you live in a world of peace, happiness, and complete freedom for all of your days. To my daughter, MaeLee Rose Essary; you were taken from this world in an hour we least expected, but you will forever be in your daddy's heart.

On June 20, 2011 a number of pre-release copies of "The Hour We Least Expected" were given to people of various backgrounds for review.

We would like to thank those who participated in this test group which include, but is not limited to the following:

Kyle Strunk
Jason Allan Jones
Kim Morse
Jarrod Morse
Meranda
Melody
Dewey Morgan
Lamps
Rhea Korte
Amanda Little
Jarrod Ritter
Bob Workman

We would like to thank our dad, Steve Essary Sr., for his support and for helping us to maintain the drive we needed to finish this project.

We would also like to thank Kim Morse for having the boldness to ask us the Big Question.

THE HOUR WE LEAST EXPECTED

Table of Contents

The Hour We Least Expected

Foreword

I admit when Steve first asked me to read this manuscript, I didn't know what to expect. It was not because I thought I would disagree with him, but because our ministries in the Gospel are so different. Mine is to minister to those that have been wounded or rejected by church and offer them hope. Steve and Aaron's is to challenge the status quo head on. I admit that makes me uncomfortable, not because I don't like to engage in a good theological debate, but because I'd rather be behind the scenes ministering to people. Both ministries are very much needed in order to set people free emotionally from the captivity we see in so many churches today. It is a partnership really. We need both generals and medics in any conflict, right? Steve and Aaron definitely have a warrior's spirit. They are like generals that do their research, form the plan of attack, and execute it flawlessly. They go after the heart of the matter, and take the message straight to those in authority that are causing the pain, and confront them with the truth.

My own grace journey initially began with an understanding of God's grace. I was challenged by a friend who called me a legalist. I had no idea what that was, but I set out to prove her wrong and found out she was right! Thank goodness because I might have gone on in that manner. I spent about a year studying and searching the Scriptures and came to a very life altering understanding of the grace of God with a solid understanding that it is His righteousness that saves and keeps us…not our own. Then one day a minister I highly respected announced that he thought everyone was going to Heaven. In my mind, I immediately dismissed him. My traitorous heart didn't quite agree with my head though because I thought about it for a few years off and on. What if it could be true? Something deep inside of me knew that it was, but it didn't line up with any of my denomination's theology. So, I pushed it down. I didn't do what Steve and Aaron did and search it out. I ran as fast as I could from it. It never left my heart though. It seemed to surface all the time. As I understood more and more about grace along my journey over the next few years, the more sense it made to me, but I couldn't say it out loud for fear someone would think I was crazy. I finally sat down one day and told my husband what I was thinking. He was so amazing. He was a licensed minister in our denomination. He should have clearly shown me the error of my ways, but instead he considered very carefully what I was saying. We both got into the Bible with fresh eyes and were amazed at what we found and amazed at how it altered the direction of our lives eventually leading us out of the mainstream church world.

Before I left my last evangelical church, I had a conversation with an old friend. See, I've known Steve Essary for a very long time. He and his brother Aaron were just teenagers when I met them. We ended up at the same church and the rest is history as they say. I knew without doubt that Steve and Aaron wanted to serve God. They wanted to see people go to Heaven. Steve was probably the most passionate person about saving the world that I've ever known personally.

One thing I've learned in my years of working with people in church is that most people don't really believe what is preached or they are seriously callous because they don't do anything about it. Steve did. He led youth ministries, camps, built youth centers…he dreamed big. I remember getting calls from Steve where he was trying as hard as he could to get the youth ministries of our area to unite to save our teens. He had this gigantic plan how to do it and wanted me to get on board. Another thing I've learned about evangelical people is that if they really do believe what they preach, they are deeply grieved emotionally by not being able to accomplish the impossible task of saving the world. I haven't met many people that fall in that category though. Most fall into the first one I talked about. Steve definitely fell into the second. Another thing I've learned in my ministry to the religiously wounded is that it is all about timing. People have to be ready to hear the gospel. I remember trying to talk to Steve about grace years ago when we were all youth leaders at the same church, but he seriously blew me off. He probably doesn't remember that now!

(*she's right! I don't remember that at all… lol…* -steve)

Anyway, fast forward to the fateful night and my comment about timing. I admit I was growing weary of being in the evangelical church world where you could not dare share a thought or a question that opposed the commonly accepted message without serious repercussions. Discipleship was a one way conversation unless questions you asked lined up with what was being taught. I was starting to feel claustrophobic, and I had begun being more open about my beliefs. One night, a few of our friends were gathered at Steve's, and he was obviously very stressed out and depressed. He was so frustrated that all his plans and efforts to save the world were not working. He was only one person and how could he get more people on board to help him save the world? This went on and on and he meant every single word of it. I can tell you that having known him for so long that I knew what he was going through because he truly believed that it was his job to save people or they would go to Hell. He was distraught over it. So, I remembered asking him a question that would alter the course of both our family's evangelical lives. I asked him something like…What if you didn't have to save the world? What if Jesus already saved the whole world? He of course freaked out on me, but he knew me. He knew my words were dangerous in evangelical circles, and I wasn't exactly comfortable throwing it out there, but I knew I had to for his sanity's sake. I haven't really talked with Steve about why I said what I did that night, but it was like a million volts of electricity were hooked up to Steve after I asked that question. I know he probably thought I was crazy, but I also knew he was my friend, and I had to tell him what, in my heart, I believed to be the truth. I had to offer him some peace…some ceasing of his labors to accomplish what I knew in my heart Jesus had already finished. You see, I believe Jesus came to this planet on a mission. He did not fail. He came on this gigantic mission to save and redeem the whole of humanity…past, present, and future. Mission accomplished. He didn't fail in any way in accomplishing that. Jesus did not say on the cross that the rest is up to you or to be continued. He said it is finished. Sharing the gospel shouldn't be some horrible fearful thing that if you say the wrong thing or, heaven forbid, don't say anything at all, you live with guilt that you couldn't reach someone. Sharing the gospel is as it is defined. Gospel literally means "good news". When you share the gospel you are sharing the good news of a completed work. Signed, sealed, and delivered. Jesus already wrapped it up for us.

In the pages that follow, you are going to go on a theological journey that is filled with passion, humor, conviction, and really solid biblical support. I know the amount of time that Steve and Aaron have put into searching the Scriptures for the information they are about to share with you. Know that is was with great sacrifice that these words are written. All of us had to give up our former identities as accepted mainstream Christians to truly read the Bible for ourselves. You may have to do that too.

Steve and Aaron have very poignantly laid out the gospel in one of the most profoundly, understandable ways that I've ever read. I couldn't be prouder of them and I definitely think the conversation that night was worth the risk I knew I was taking.

Steve and Aaron…well done.

Kim Morse
Fellow recovering CAM member as Steve and Aaron call it

THE HOUR WE LEAST EXPECTED

CHAPTER 1

AN UNSOLVED MYSTERY

I was a little hesitant to accept the invitation, after all 5am was very early to get up on a Saturday. "That sounds like fun, I will see you there" was the last thing I said as I hung up the phone and climbed into bed. What was I getting myself into? I just finished a big job and instead of sleeping in the next day, I was setting my alarm clock for an even earlier time than usual. I just hoped that my friend was right and that tomorrow would not be a big disappointment.

Trying desperately to fall asleep fast, my mind drifted to many various places. I wondered if Ms. King was happy with the work we did to her house. That thought led me to remember that I forgot to put the knobs on her vanity cabinet in the hall bathroom. "Oh well, I thought I was done with that job", I thought as I began to go room to room in my mind searching for anything else I needed to finish that I might have forgot.

I rolled over and reached for the floor with my left hand, searching the carpet for my phone, so I could put a reminder in my calendar. I was very disappointed when I picked it up and realized that it was already 1:43am. I was so tempted to cancel, but he had been asking me forever to go, so I rolled back over and made another attempt to sleep.

“I wonder if Ms. King is a Christian”, was the very next thought I had. Luckily, Mr. Sandman came in when he did, because it was those types of thoughts that would normally keep me awake for the rest of the night.

“BEEP!!! BEEP!!! BEEP!!! BEEP!!!”

Seriously? 4:15 already?

Dwayne was already packed and waiting as I pulled up in his driveway at 4:59. He was obviously excited about our short trip. We quickly loaded my truck and headed for the country.

Several times I thought we were lost as he led me down what seemed like a dozen or more twisty, narrow, gravel roads.

“Ok, turn left here by these railroad tracks” he said.

“You mean by this sign that says No Trespassing?” I said as I shook my head and pressed the gas pedal, propelling us down the dirt path, through the deep mud holes and around the tree line.

Out of view of the road, we unloaded our cargo and prepared our coolers.

“Where is the water?” I asked, looking in every direction.

“It’s just over there” he said, pointing past the tall hill that the railroad tracks ran on. “We have to carry the boat.”

Did I mention how tired I was? Sighing with dread, we loaded the rest of our supplies inside and I grabbed my end of the 12’ aluminum boat and we began to climb the rocky hill to the tracks.

Just as we reached the peak and set the boat down to rest, I looked over the hill where two deer were eating blackberries. I motioned to Dwayne to look, but as I did, they saw me and bolted in an instant. He barely caught their white tails as they hopped the fence and disappeared. I have to admit that although I was worn out from working and not sleeping, that made me smile. We were so close to them.

We took a few more breaths and returned to our chore. "He never told me about this part" I thought as we walked 200 feet north down the railroad tracks and then 50 feet east down the hill on the other side, 100 feet back south through the shallow creek then back up one more treacherous hill.

"Can you see the water?" he asked as we exited the wooded landscape into a massive field.

I was too out of breath to answer, so I nodded my head as we walked the remaining 500 feet to the water's edge.

We each prepared our fishing poles with weights and hooks. We arranged all of our gear and decided who would sit where and then we launched out on the water.

As Dwayne paddled us to the first area he wanted us to try, I was admiring the beauty of this hole in the Earth.

The water was so clear, I could see down 12 feet or more. I had never been fishing anywhere but muddy old ponds, so I was thrilled to get to see dozens of fish swimming as we glided above them.

I saw largemouth bass, blue gills, turtles, and even a snake. There was a heron off in the distance walking in the shallow water near the bank. I saw three vultures circling in the air to the west of us. There were frogs croaking and crickets chirping and many birds singing. Then it was all interrupted by the blast of the horn from the coal train as it made us all very aware of its arrival.

Once the train finally passed and I could hear myself think again, I asked Dwayne, "Where do you suppose all of this came from?"

Dwayne and I had been friends for a long time, so he knew just what I meant.

"I suppose there may have been some sort of huge explosion around 100 billion years ago and once all of the dust settled, this stuff just started growing" he said as he cast his bait under a nearby tree that was growing out of the cliff in front of us.

I laughed as I said "I'm sure you're right."

We caught several nice bass that day and more bluegill than we could count, but the best part for me was the long conversation we had that started with some jokes about evolution, and led to all sorts of things, from Heaven to Hell, the Garden of Eden, the New Heaven and Earth, the coming end of the world and all of the people in our lives that we were not sure would be included when Jesus came back to take us all home to Heaven.

He was right. I had a blast that day. I am glad I went.

Who is right?

The conversation Dwayne and I had that day was one I have had many times in my life. I could never understand how anyone could believe that this world just popped up out of nowhere and now we live on it. Not only are we talking about simple, single celled organisms becoming super complex beings with intellectual thoughts and complicated emotions, but also we must consider all of the other living things that spawned from nothing to support us.

For example, how did Evolution know to create honey bees at the same time as everything else? What I mean is, without honey bees, many of the foods we eat today would not grow. So what did we eat in the first place? Did that first cell that sprung to life eat dirt? Everything on this planet seems to be connected and dependent upon something else, so how is it possible that Evolution did it all by chance. That Evolution must be one lucky guy to pull all of this off in any amount of time.

At the same time, I have to admit that I was not here six thousand years ago, so I cannot testify that I saw the God of the Bible speak this place into being. I didn't write the Bible. I have never written anything until now, so all I can do is think about things and try to figure out what makes sense to me.

Was the Earth created by God?

How much is this question worth, and can I phone a friend for help?

As much as I would like to say that God did create the entire universe in 6 days, exactly as the book of Genesis describes, I must admit that it is a mystery. I have always believed it was true, but I do not have any real evidence to support my claims. Some creationists claim to have hard evidence but so do some evolutionists.

To be honest, I am no longer interested in the debate, because of the simple reason that both sides claim their case as facts.

In some elementary schools, evolution and the age of our

planet is taught as a fact. In some Christian schools, creation is taught as a fact. What is wrong with presenting both sides of the story?

Fear of the wrong side winning is my guess as to why we cannot seem to let people make up their own minds. The evolutionists believe their theory, so they teach it as fact, hoping that someday it will just be accepted without question. Creationists do the same.

When looking at the argument from both sides, I can now see why each is so militant in their tactics. Evolutionists are often atheist and do not believe in God. (At least that is my perception, so just go with me here.) They see religion as a worthless set of rules that are holding people back from making significant contributions to society. Christians believe that our eternal destination is dependent upon our choice to believe the message of the Bible and act on those beliefs, so of course they must be forward. Neither side can afford to give up ground, so neither side seems willing to even consider any evidence put forth by the opposition.

So what would happen if Christians and evolutionists actually talked and tried to understand each other? Would the results be catastrophic? Would the creationist change his mind if he heard a convincing argument? Would the atheist fall to his knees and worship God if he admitted that the other side had a good point? Although I am sure there are exceptions to this rule, both sides seem to think that bashing each other in the head would be the best way to settle the argument. They might be right. ☺

Unsolved Mysteries

No matter what you believe about the beginnings of our planet and/or species, one thing is for sure. It is an unsolved mystery.

Will we ever know?

Maybe… Maybe not…

I do believe, however, that we will not get any closer to knowing anything without further investigation. I'm not talking about further collection of one-sided evidence, but rather we need to be truth seekers and start looking for the truth, no matter what we may find.

It takes time to solve mysteries. I believe there is an answer to every question and the truth is the truth no matter who believes it. But some truths remain unknown.

The Bible says…

Whether you believe that the Bible is the inspired word of God or just a collection of fairy tales, it does exist. I own several copies in fact. I have 18 different translations of it on my computer. I read it all the time, and I have frequent conversations about it with other people all the time. You could never ever convince me that it doesn't exist.

As a matter of fact, I have never heard one person suggest that it doesn't exist.

So, if you think about it, we all finally have something we can agree on.

The Bible exists!!!

But what does it say?

Now there is a can of worms for you. Try asking that question to the next 100 people you come across and see what they all say.

Believe it or not, even most atheists have read the Bible and have an opinion as to what the overall message is all about.

Although there are over 30,000 different Christian denominations, most Christians will tell you that they know exactly what the message of the Bible is. Are they all correct? They are all different, so what does that tell you?

Evolution is Real!!!

The way the Bible has been taught has been evolving since it was first put together. It cracks me up when people now say to us that we are questioning a 2000 year old message. The message contained in the Bible is an unsolved mystery. As a matter of fact, the book has not even been in distribution for much more than 500 years. Before that, the Catholic priests pretty much had the only copies, and they did not believe that the common people would be able to understand it, so they kept it to themselves. It wasn't until a man named Martin Luther stood up to what was in that day the "Currently Accepted Message" or CAM as we call it. Today's mainstream Christian church is the result of Luther's Protestant Reformation.

I'm not going to bore you with the details of this reformation, but I just want to make the point that what you hear in church today is not what you would have heard 500, 200, or even 100 years ago.

Why?

Did the message change? Did the Bible change???

No…

Our understanding of that message is changing.

Is that good?

Most church leaders will tell you that it is important to learn your Bible, (as they teach it), well and always stick to your guns. They will warn you to stay away from differing opinions, as they might lead you astray.

Don't they understand that Martin Luther's differing opinion is what ended the mess we were in before?

Differing opinions are not dangerous.

Being close-minded is very dangerous.

Adolph Hitler was close-minded. He believed his way was the only right way and decided that it would be best to rid the world of anyone not like him.

The Big Question

In early 2007, I sat down in a chair near a very close friend of mine. She was the Youth Pastor at the church I was attending. I had been a Youth Pastor myself and I was very interested in helping her build her ministry up.

"What do we need to do to win more kids to Christ?" I asked her.

With much hesitation, she proceeded to ask me the biggest question I have ever heard in my life.

"Do you think it is possible that the message contained in the Bible is that Jesus saved the entire world and nobody is going to Hell?"

She followed her question with various clarifying statements, but I can't remember anything else about the conversation we had that day. All I remember is getting very frustrated and very angry. I stood up and began my usual nervous habit of pacing.

I proceeded to scold her and explain to her how important our job, as Christians, was and how disappointed I was in her ability to fall of the wagon so easily and… Wow!!! I was mad!!!

I ended my rant with a promise. I was going to write a short essay to prove she was wrong.

"The nerve of some people…" I thought as I paced my way to my room and fired up my computer.

How could she say that? We have been in the same church for years!!! She was the Youth Pastor for crying out loud. Had she never read the Bible?

I opened my computer Bible program and began to read. I knew exactly where to go to find the evidence I needed to support my claim, yet when I got there, the passage no longer seemed so clear cut. I spent 3 hours that night, trying desperately to find some hardcore evidence to stop her in her tracks. The next day I approached my brother with the chore I had now undertaken and he agreed to help.

2 weeks and over 80 combined hours of feverish Bible study later, I took a deep breath and paused my brain. Why was it so hard to prove she was wrong? Every preacher I have told this story to has agreed with me that it should really be very easy to prove she was wrong, so why was I having so much trouble?

It was at this point that I did what I hope that many of you will eventually do. I prayed to God for the truth. I had been praying to God to help me prove my point, but this time, I approached Him in a different manner.

"God… I am no longer worried about trying to prove my point. All I ask is that you now show me the truth. If I have been right all this time, then you can show me and I will continue to preach it until I die. But if I am wrong, please show me the truth and no matter how much of a fool I will seem to my friends and the world, I will change my mind and preach what you show me."

In Acts 17:11, the Bereans are praised for being open-minded and considering the new thoughts and ideas that were being presented to them. It is often looked down upon when someone in the Christian world begins to talk differently than the rest of the group. I am by no means suggesting that you take every new thing you hear and believe it, but at least be willing to see that you do not know everything already.

To know everything is to be like God Himself. Do you know everything? Do you have it all figured out? Obviously some people think they do. Do you?

I used to think I knew exactly what the Bible had to say, that is until I tried to answer the big question. It was then that I realized that I didn't know anything. It was then that I realized that my brain was stuck in a loop that was unending. You see, once you stop learning, you stop recording, and your brain starts running the loop until you sound like a broken record.

The Hour We Least Expected

According to the Bible, approximately two thousand years ago there was born a Man named Jesus. He made many claims about Himself. He claimed to be the Son of God. He said He was here to save the world from the punishment for their sins. He said He would finish the work that His Father, God, had begun. He talked a lot about sin, death, and the end of the world. One day, His followers asked Him when He would finish His work and what the End would be like. He told them it would happen in an hour they least expected. To this day many look for this hour with fear and anticipation because He said it would be like a thief coming in the night.

The Hour We Least Expected is the moment in time where everything will change. Although no one will know the hour before it happens, will we recognize that hour after it has come and gone? Obviously the Christian community believes that the changes that will take place will be highly visible, so much that the entire world will definitely know within moments of it happening. But remember that although the Bible prophesied the coming Messiah, very few recognized Him. And Jesus often talked very plainly about His coming death and yet the disciples all seemed so shocked when it happened.

The end of the world is a mystery that everyone seems to be interested in. Will it happen like we have been taught? Or when the mystery is finally revealed, will we find out that what was prophesied wasn't anything like we thought it would be?

The Currently Accepted Message or CAM

In the coming chapters, we will examine a set of doctrines that seems to be common in today's mainstream Christian churches. The CAM or currently accepted message is always changing, as it should be. The mysteries in the Bible continue to be solved over time, so it is fitting that as we discover new truths, that we should review them and change our thinking accordingly. If this did not happen, we would all be buying our way into heaven as was common before Martin Luther's Protestant Reformation in the 1500's.

Today's CAM teaches several things that we have always subscribed to. In 2007, however, we were forced to reexamine these common ideas and the conclusions we finally came to are astounding. We will be examining the following common CAM beliefs and teachings:

- Does the Bible say that you must believe in Jesus to go to Heaven when you die?
- And that your eternal destination is your personal choice?
- And that the Earth will be physically destroyed in the future?
- And that those who do not meet certain requirements will burn in a lake of fire forever?

The Hour We Least Expected

Chapter 2

Do You Now Believe?

As we said in Chapter 1, although there are so many different versions of Christianity, there are a few ideas that seem to be consistent throughout the faith. Probably the most popular among these is the belief that a person is "saved" from the punishment for their sins if they have personally made the choice to believe in Jesus.

In this chapter, we are going to examine this idea and other ideas that are closely related to it.

Our existence in a nutshell…

According to the account in Genesis, God created ALL things that are in existence. In six days, He created the Earth and the sky and all of the living creatures in the ocean and on land. He made all of the flowers we look at and the fruit that we eat.

Somewhere in the middle of this new world, He made a special garden called "Eden" and in this Garden of Eden, He placed His favorite creation, man. He named this man "Adam" and He made Adam a companion and Adam called her “Eve”.

They lived in this garden where they had everything they could ever want or need. They could do whatever they wanted to do, with the exception of one thing. God had placed a certain tree in the midst of the garden. It was called the tree of “the knowledge of good and evil”. God gave them one commandment, and that was to NOT eat the fruit of that tree.

If they did eat of that tree, God had warned them that they would die.

Being that they were made to be creatures with a free will, they became very curious about this tree, and with a little persuasion from a certain snake in the grass, they disobeyed God’s command and ate the fruit. Instantly they experienced a change in their minds and bodies. They suddenly realized that they were naked and they became ashamed.

They hid themselves from God and when He discovered what had happened, He made them leave the garden. This event is commonly referred to as man’s “fall” from the garden. Not only were they made to leave the garden, but now there seemed to be a disconnection between them and God that they could not repair. Life was very different for them as they now had to work hard every day just to survive.

As time passed by, they had children and their children had children and this condition of “sin” (disobedience to God) became worse and worse. Murder, theft, rape, adultery, and many other sinful acts became more and more common.

Although mankind had the ability to do whatever they wanted, there was always a desire to become close to God again.

Many generations later, God made a covenant with a man named Moses. This covenant is called "The Law". The Law was a list of rules or commandments that must be followed in order to regain the righteousness that was lost by Adam.

If anyone could not keep all of the commandments of the law, certain animal sacrifices would be made by the priest and the person's sins would be forgiven. In time, it became obvious that no man could keep this covenant with God because it was very difficult if not impossible. Many tried and ALL failed.

God, being a very loving Father, would not settle for the evident outcome so He made a promise to man.

Sprinkled throughout the Old Testament there are many prophesies that all state that one day God would send to us a Savior. This Savior would save us from the penalties of sin.

For hundreds of reasons that we will not be discussing in this book, this Savior is believed by us to be Jesus of Nazareth.

Jesus lived up to the standards of the Law which is something no one else was ever able to accomplish. Although He did nothing wrong, the religious leaders hated Him and had Him arrested.

He stood trial and, even though his judge found no fault with Him, He was sentenced to die by the option of His own people. They beat Him, stripped Him, and spit in His face but despite all of this He only loved them. They made Him carry His own cross up a long treacherous hill where they nailed Him to it and lifted Him up to die.

While He was on the cross the sun went black and the moon did not shine for three hours. Then as He took his final breath there was a great earthquake and not too far from there, the curtain that separated the priests from the "Holy of Holies" hung in the temple ripped in two.

Those that loved Him took and wrapped His body and placed Him in a tomb. Three days later, still very sorrowful, they came to visit his tomb. To their surprise, the stone that covered the entrance had been rolled away and the tomb was empty. He appeared to many for several days after this and then He ascended to heaven where He sits at God's right hand.

Where our differences begin…

This much of the story is generally agreed upon. There were several eye witnesses to confirm these physical events, but like many stories, it is what happened behind the scenes that really matters and this is where we now disagree with the CAM or "Currently Accepted Message".

We agree that, while Jesus was on the cross, the sins of the world were placed upon Him. He paid the penalty for the sins of every man and woman that ever was and ever would be, therefore restoring the righteousness or "right standing" that we lost in the garden.

Here is where the differences come into play.

CAM members will tell you that although Jesus paid your debt, it is still your responsibility to "accept" this free gift He has given.

They say it is like a car that, although it has been given to you, you have to pick up the keys and drive it for it to be of any use to you. The way this is said sounds logical and therefore is easily accepted as the truth. There are many passages in the Bible that also seem to support this idea and we are going to take a close look at these and see if we can understand the reasoning of the CAM.

The first verse that comes to mind to most CAM members is definitely the most famous and most quoted verse in the Bible. In fact, it was the first verse I was ever taught to memorize as a child. It is ***John 3:16...***

> ***For God so loved the world that He gave His only begotten Son, that whoever believes in Him should not perish but have everlasting life.***

Their explanation of this verse seems to make very good sense, and to the surprise of many, we agree with their explanation, mostly.

Whoever believes in Jesus will have everlasting life and whoever does not will perish.

We cannot deny that this is what this verse means, but shortly in this chapter we will explain that there is a hidden meaning to this thought and in order to fully understand what Jesus meant we cannot stop reading the book of John right here at chapter 3. There are many more chapters to John's book and this issue of the need for belief in Jesus carries on through every one of them. You will see very soon what we mean.

Another commonly used verse that is used to show the need for our belief and acceptance in and of Jesus is ***Romans 10:9...***

> ***that if you confess with your mouth the Lord Jesus and believe in your heart that God has raised Him from the dead, you will be saved.***

When read alone, this verse does appear to give weight to their idea that belief and acceptance is required. Like John 3:16, however, this verse is not alone and later in this chapter, we will show you very clearly what the writer meant when he penned this passage.

One more verse we will deal with in this chapter is ***2Corinthians 5:17...***

Therefore, if anyone is in Christ, he is a new creation; old things have passed away; behold, all things have become new.

The use of the word "if" in this passage does seem to lend to the idea that there are some that are not "in Christ". Again, we will explain that this passage, when read with the rest of the chapter in which it was included, actually makes a very different claim than what has been commonly accepted.

The Trump verse: John 3:16

We call John 3:16 the "Trump" verse because, in almost every debate we have with CAM members, this one verse is pulled out very early in hopes that it will end the discussion quickly. What our friends find out next is that we have considered this verse and have actually spent a great deal of time looking into the meaning of it.

Before we reveal the hidden meaning to John 3:16, we are going to first point out that belief is NOT the only requirement that Jesus talked about.

Requirements and Disqualification

Many times in the New Testament the subject of eternal life came up as different people would ask Jesus how to obtain it. Let's look at some of these passages and see what Jesus had to say about the matter. First let's look at ***Matthew 19:16-22...***

Now behold, one came and said to Him, "Good Teacher, what good thing shall I do that I may have eternal life?" So He said to him, "Why do you call Me good? No one is good but One, that is, God. But if you want to enter into life, keep the commandments." He said to Him, "Which ones?" Jesus said, " 'YOU SHALL NOT MURDER,' 'YOU SHALL NOT COMMIT ADULTERY,' 'YOU SHALL NOT STEAL,' 'YOU SHALL NOT BEAR FALSE WITNESS,' 'HONOR YOUR FATHER AND YOUR MOTHER,' and, 'YOU SHALL LOVE YOUR NEIGHBOR AS YOURSELF.' " The young man said to Him, "All these things I have kept from my youth. What do I still lack?" Jesus said to him, "If you want to be perfect, go, sell what you have and give to the poor, and you will have treasure in heaven; and come, follow Me." But when the young man heard that saying, he went away sorrowful, for he had great possessions.

Here Jesus tells this man that he must follow the commandments.

If belief in Jesus is the only requirement, then why didn't Jesus tell him that all he had to do was believe?

Did Jesus not want this man to have eternal life?

Then the man tells Jesus that he has kept the commands and Jesus goes and makes the requirements harder on him by suggesting something that the man was unwilling to do.

Something just doesn't seem right here.

Even the disciples were bewildered by this. Look what they say next and how Jesus answers them in ***Matthew 19:25-26...***

When His disciples heard it, they were greatly

astonished, saying, "Who then can be saved?" But Jesus looked at them and said to them, "With men this is impossible, but with God all things are possible."

"Who then can be saved?" they ask.

Why does Jesus tell them that with men this is impossible?

According to the CAM, it is the choice of men to believe and accept Jesus to be saved.

Why didn't Jesus explain that belief in Him was the only way?

Did He not want them to believe?

Was belief in Him impossible for them? Hmmm…

Jesus did in fact just tell the young man to obey the commands to gain eternal life and this requirement cannot be ignored.

Let's look at other requirements Jesus mentions in His teachings. ***John 3:1-15...***

There was a man of the Pharisees named Nicodemus, a ruler of the Jews. This man came to Jesus by night and said to Him, "Rabbi, we know that You are a teacher come from God; for no one can do these signs that You do unless God is with him." Jesus answered and said to him, "Most assuredly, I say to you, unless one is born again, he cannot see the kingdom of God." Nicodemus said to Him, "How can a man be born when he is old? Can he enter a second time into his mother's womb and be born?" Jesus answered, "Most assuredly, I say to you, unless one is born of water and the Spirit, he cannot enter the kingdom of God. That which is born of the flesh is flesh, and that which is born

of the Spirit is spirit. Do not marvel that I said to you, 'You must be born again.' The wind blows where it wishes, and you hear the sound of it, but cannot tell where it comes from and where it goes. So is everyone who is born of the Spirit." Nicodemus answered and said to Him, "How can these things be?" Jesus answered and said to him, "Are you the teacher of Israel, and do not know these things? Most assuredly, I say to you, We speak what We know and testify what We have seen, and you do not receive Our witness. If I have told you earthly things and you do not believe, how will you believe if I tell you heavenly things? No one has ascended to heaven but He who came down from heaven, that is, the Son of Man who is in heaven. And as Moses lifted up the serpent in the wilderness, even so must the Son of Man be lifted up, that whoever believes in Him should not perish but have eternal life.

Here, in John 3:3, Jesus explains to Nicodemus that in order to see or enter in to God's kingdom one must be "born again". We will explain this more in the next chapter, but for now we just want to note a few things.

If you read this whole passage in John 3, you will find that Jesus never clearly explains what being "born again" means or how to make it happen.

This makes us question again, why does Jesus give the requirement of being born again to Nicodemus but not the requirement of obeying the commands?

Why didn't Jesus tell the rich young ruler that he needs to be born again?

Why does Jesus give so many different requirements to so many different people but never all of them to any one of them?

The fact is that Jesus is giving us hints of something bigger going on behind the scenes. We are starting to see a pattern that we call "requirements and disqualification." Jesus gives a requirement then demonstrates to the one He gives it to how he or she is disqualified by the requirement.

As this story pertains to belief, Nicodemus comes professing that Jesus must be of God since He was able to do all of the miracles that he saw Jesus do.

Without any regard to Nicodemus' remarks, Jesus immediately throws him a curve ball and teaches him something that he cannot understand. Again, when asked to clarify the meaning and the mechanism of being born again, Jesus tells him that he cannot understand it because it is a heavenly thing, like the wind blowing wherever it will and on whomever it will.

Jesus sends him away bewildered, puzzled and unsatisfied.

Did He want to confuse Nicodemus? Again, why didn't He tell him to simply believe in Him? Why is there always more to it or another requirement added to the list? Let's move on.

Look here in ***John 5:28-29...***

> ***Do not marvel at this; for the hour is coming in which all who are in the graves will hear His voice and come forth— those who have done good, to the resurrection of life, and those who have done evil, to the resurrection of condemnation.***

Here Jesus says that He will judge the dead according to whether they have done good or practiced evil.

How many of the dead do you think never practiced evil?

He is saying that they will be judged according to the Law.

Once again, this statement demonstrates that the gift of eternal life is dependent on a person's ability to live according to the Law.

This was hard enough as it was, but look at what Jesus says here in ***Matthew 5:21-22...***

You have heard that it was said to those of old, 'YOU SHALL NOT MURDER, and whoever murders will be in danger of the judgment.' But I say to you that whoever is angry with his brother without a cause shall be in danger of the judgment. And whoever says to his brother, 'Raca!' shall be in danger of the council. But whoever says, 'You fool!' shall be in danger of hell fire.

We will be explaining the "judgment" and "hell fire" in the coming chapters, but for now, let's focus on the increased difficulty that Jesus brings to the commandment against murder. Here, Jesus explains that anger with others is enough to be found guilty of breaking the Law. ***Matthew 5:27-28...***

"You have heard that it was said to those of old, 'YOU SHALL NOT COMMIT ADULTERY.' But I say to you that whoever looks at a woman to lust for her has already committed adultery with her in his heart.

Jesus was teaching the Law as the requirement for eternal life, and not just the written law, but the full intent of the law.

What we are pointing out here is that belief is not the only requirement Jesus mentions.

So how can the CAM say belief is the only way when Christ so clearly says otherwise?

Once again there is something deeper happening here, about which we will get to momentarily. Let's examine a few more requirements. ***John 6:50-58...***

This is the bread which comes down from heaven, that one may eat of it and not die. I am the living bread which came down from heaven. If anyone eats of this bread, he will live forever; and the bread that I shall give is My flesh, which I shall give for the life of the world." The Jews therefore quarreled among themselves, saying, "How can this Man give us His flesh to eat?" Then Jesus said to them, "Most assuredly, I say to you, unless you eat the flesh of the Son of Man and drink His blood, you have no life in you. Whoever eats My flesh and drinks My blood has eternal life, and I will raise him up at the last day. For My flesh is food indeed, and My blood is drink indeed. He who eats My flesh and drinks My blood abides in Me, and I in him. As the living Father sent Me, and I live because of the Father, so he who feeds on Me will live because of Me. This is the bread which came down from heaven—not as your fathers ate the manna, and are dead. He who eats this bread will live forever."

Looking back on Jesus' words it is easy for us to see that He was speaking metaphorically. The Jews of the day, however, did not understand this. Jesus told them that they would have to eat His flesh and drink His blood in order to obtain eternal life. The word continues on to show how this saying offended many. ***John 6:59-66...***

These things He said in the synagogue as He taught in Capernaum. Therefore many of His disciples, when they heard this, said, "This is a hard saying; who can understand it?" When Jesus knew in Himself that His disciples complained about this, He said to them,

"Does this offend you? What then if you should see the Son of Man ascend where He was before? It is the Spirit who gives life; the flesh profits nothing. The words that I speak to you are spirit, and they are life. But there are some of you who do not believe." For Jesus knew from the beginning who they were who did not believe, and who would betray Him. And He said, "Therefore I have said to you that no one can come to Me unless it has been granted to him by My Father." From that time many of His disciples went back and walked with Him no more.

So again, Jesus gives a requirement that no one was willing to fulfill and by doing so many went away and did not follow Him anymore.

Why on earth would Jesus not clarify to these people what He means when He says all of this? If belief was so important why did He chase so many away with His teachings? Did He not love them enough to give them a real chance? Could He not explain to them what He really meant?

He has already said the requirements to gain eternal life are to obey the commands, sell all and give to the poor, become born again (without explanation), and now eat His flesh and drink His blood?

The CAM will tell you that in order to get to Heaven, you must believe in Jesus.

If you ask them why, they will tell you "because Jesus said you must" (in accordance with John 3:16), but like we said before, the CAM cannot say that we only have to believe when Christ not only mentions belief but specifically mentions these other requirements as the means in which mankind was to obtain eternal life.

So why don't we hear CAM members teaching the Law as Jesus did?

Most CAM members believe that we do not live according to the Old Covenant, or the Law, any longer, but we now live by the New Covenant, or Grace, that was given to us by Jesus. Then they will say that the only requirement, for that Grace to be applied to your life, is to believe in Him, because He said that you must.

So again, our point is that you cannot point out Jesus words concerning belief, but ignore ALL of the other requirements that He speaks of.

There is a mystery here. It is not easy to understand, but once you see it, you will know it is true.

Could They Believe?

So the point we are trying to make here is that Jesus says that the requirements that must be met in order to receive eternal life go way beyond belief. That means that believing in Jesus cannot be the only thing that we must do to get eternal life.

So if we cannot fulfill all of the other requirements that Jesus mentions, can we really fulfill the belief requirement?

Could the disciples?

They were the ones who walked right beside Him day in and day out. If anyone could truly believe in Him it would be them, right? Let's finish this passage found in ***John 6:67-71...***

Then Jesus said to the twelve, "Do you also want to go away?" But Simon Peter answered Him, "Lord, to whom shall we go? You have the words of eternal life. Also we have come to believe and know that You are the

Christ, the Son of the living God." Jesus answered them, "Did I not choose you, the twelve, and one of you is a devil?" He spoke of Judas Iscariot, the son of Simon, for it was he who would betray Him, being one of the twelve.

Notice Jesus' response when Peter tells Him that they, the twelve, believe in Him. He sharply points out that He chose them on purpose and that one of them was even a devil thus really saying that He knows that they do not believe in Him.

We will show you that He mentions this over and over as we move forward through the rest of this chapter. He often says "you must believe…" and then "but you do not"

The Work of Belief

Look at what the Apostle Paul says in ***Ephesians 2:8-9...***

For by grace you are saved through faith, and that not of yourselves, it is the gift of God, not of works, lest anyone should boast.

Paul says that we are saved by grace, not of works or deeds or keeping the law, but by grace only.

So if we cannot get to heaven by keeping the law why did Jesus teach this as a requirement in some places, but in John 3 he teaches about belief only?

This seems very peculiar, as does this next verse... ***John 6:28-29...***

Then they said to Him, "What shall we do, that we may work the works of God?" Jesus answered and said to them, "This is the work of God, that you believe in Him whom He sent."

In this passage, Jesus tells them that belief in Him is a work. This may not seem like a big deal to many readers, but after hearing your whole life that you are saved by grace and NOT through works we have become sensitive to this kind of statement.

So is believing in Jesus a "work"?

Every CAM member I have debated with before writing this book, says no.

They say we are saved by faith and not works, but then we see Jesus say that believing in Him is work, it seems a little ironic. As a matter of fact, they look shocked when I ask this question, or when I sometimes just suggest this to be the case. But seriously, is belief in Him a work?

It seems that if it were not a work that it should be something that is easy to do, right?

If it is so easy, then why did the disciples have so much trouble accomplishing this? After all, they were with Him constantly. They saw with their own two eyes the miracles He did, yet Jesus says that they don't believe. How is this possible?

If you read the book of James you will find that faith without works is dead. What does that mean? It means that actions speak louder than words. The disciples told Jesus several times that they believed, and He responded to them the same way each time, including this time in ***John 16:29-32...***

His disciples said to Him, "See, now You are speaking plainly, and using no figure of speech! Now we are sure that You know all things, and have no need that anyone should question You. By this we believe that

You came forth from God." Jesus answered them, "Do you now believe? Indeed the hour is coming, yes, has now come, that you will be scattered, each to his own, and will leave Me alone. And yet I am not alone, because the Father is with Me.

So you see, merely saying that you believe is not good enough. Your actions have to follow suit. The disciples cast out demons and healed people too, yet Jesus said that their level of faith was not enough.

Why?

Because the requirement was actually **faith without doubt** which is something that was impossible for them?

You see, if one really believes without doubt then obeying all of the commandments like selling all you have and giving it to the poor and leaving everything behind would be easy.

So why would Jesus set the standard so impossibly high, as if the law wasn't hard enough?

Let's look ahead just a little at a passage that deals with belief and works of the law in regards to the end times. ***Matthew 7:22-23...***

Many will say to Me in that day, 'Lord, Lord, have we not prophesied in Your name, cast out demons in Your name, and done many wonders in Your name?' And then I will declare to them, 'I never knew you; depart from Me, you who practice lawlessness!'

How could anyone who has the ability to prophesy and to cast out demons not believe?

Nonbelievers, in the terms of the CAM, would not even

know to do such a thing would they?

So even supernatural practices cannot be counted as proof of believing to the extent that Jesus' requirement of belief demands. The fact that Jesus explains this to His disciples not too long before he sends them out to cast out devils is also a hint of something else going on that we will explain more throughout this book.

They Could Not Believe

There is another reason they had trouble believing. This one, at first, seemed to be even more unusual to me. Look here in ***Matthew 13:34-35...***

> ***All these things Jesus spoke to the multitude in parables; and without a parable He did not speak to them, that it might be fulfilled which was spoken by the prophet, saying: "I WILL OPEN MY MOUTH IN PARABLES; I WILL UTTER THINGS KEPT SECRET FROM THE FOUNDATION OF THE WORLD."***

Jesus ALWAYS taught in parables about things that were kept secret from the beginning of time. I was taught in Sunday school that Jesus used this form of teaching so that people would better understand what He was trying to tell them. That is not even close to the case though. Look at this passage in ***Matthew 13:13-15...***

> ***Therefore I speak to them in parables, because seeing they do not see, and hearing they do not hear, nor do they understand. And in them the prophecy of Isaiah is fulfilled, which says: 'HEARING YOU WILL HEAR AND SHALL NOT UNDERSTAND, AND SEEING YOU WILL SEE AND NOT PERCEIVE; FOR THE HEARTS OF THIS PEOPLE HAVE GROWN DULL.***

THEIR EARS ARE HARD OF HEARING, AND THEIR EYES THEY HAVE CLOSED, LEST THEY SHOULD SEE WITH THEIR EYES AND HEAR WITH THEIR EARS, LEST THEY SHOULD UNDERSTAND WITH THEIR HEARTS AND TURN, SO THAT I SHOULD HEAL THEM.'

This passage suggests that Jesus taught in parables TO CONFUSE THEM!

Why would He want to confuse them?

Does He *not* want them to believe? It sure does not seem like it would benefit anyone not to believe. Check out this very similar passage in ***John 12: 37-41...***

But although He had done so many signs before them, they did not believe in Him, that the word of Isaiah the prophet might be fulfilled, which he spoke: "LORD, WHO HAS BELIEVED OUR REPORT? AND TO WHOM HAS THE ARM OF THE LORD BEEN REVEALED?" Therefore they could not believe, because Isaiah said again: "HE HAS BLINDED THEIR EYES AND HARDENED THEIR HEARTS, LEST THEY SHOULD SEE WITH THEIR EYES, LEST THEY SHOULD UNDERSTAND WITH THEIR HEARTS AND TURN, SO THAT I SHOULD HEAL THEM." These things Isaiah said when he saw His glory and spoke of Him.

Why would God blind their eyes and harden their hearts and keep them from believing?

It seems that there is a bit of bad tag teaming going on here that, at first glance, doesn't make sense.

On one hand we have Jesus saying that belief is a must, and

on the other hand we have God with His big hands covering their eyes so that it is impossible to believe.

What is wrong with this picture?

The answer is nothing!

There is a very good reason that God had for keeping people in the dark which we are about to point out.

It is a mystery, a secret kept from the beginning of time.

Not everything in the Bible is cut and dry.

Many Christians read the Bible and pick up on the first thing that comes to mind, just like when we read John 3:16. This verse makes it sound like a very bad thing to be caught not believing, but like much of the Bible, the meanings to these words are hidden just barely out of reach.

It takes an open mind and "out of the box" thinking to dig a little deeper and search the meanings of the text.

Keep reading, because it will all make sense really soon.

Was Belief a Requirement Before or After the Cross?

Some CAM members say that the "other" requirements for gaining eternal life were taught because the people were still under the Law since Jesus had not given them the New Covenant yet. They say that now the only requirement left of all of the law is to believe. We agree that until Jesus died people were under the Law, but look how Jesus worded this in ***John 3:18...***

He who believes in Him is not condemned; but he who does not believe is condemned <u>already</u>, because

he has not believed in the name of the only begotten Son of God.

Here Jesus says that whoever doesn't believe is condemned already.

But this is long before the cross.

Why doesn't He say that AFTER the cross, they will have an opportunity to believe?

Look at this in ***John 5:24...***

"Most assuredly, I say to you, he who hears My word and believes in Him who sent Me has everlasting life, and shall not come into judgment, but has passed from death into life.

Here Jesus says "passed" as in past tense, as in it has already happened.

Again, this is before the cross.

He is saying that if one believed in Him, even prior to the events of the cross, then they would have passed from death to life already.

What would happen if one was to believe in Jesus before He died on the cross?

Jesus is telling them they must believe or else.

What if they did?

You see, none of them even knew He was going to die yet. All they heard was "The Kingdom of God is coming" and "You must believe".

He never said, “After I die, you must believe”, in fact, He was already telling them that it was too late.

He also did not say anything to clear up the matter like “After I die, then the belief requirement will be the only one that remains.”

Like we said earlier, it is a mystery and the answers are in the details.

The Mystery is Revealed

In John 7 and 8, Jesus gives us some very good hints as to how this whole thing is going to go down. Up until now, we have seen over and over that Jesus was telling them that they had better believe, or they would perish. Even though belief was so stressed to them, Jesus always concluded that their level of belief was not enough to qualify them. ***John 7:33-34...***

Then Jesus said to them, "I shall be with you a little while longer, and then I go to Him who sent Me. You will seek Me and not find Me, and where I am you cannot come."

This statement made them wonder what He meant. Where was He going? Why couldn’t they go? Again in ***John 8:21-24...***

Then Jesus said to them again, "I am going away, and you will seek Me, and will die in your sin. Where I go you cannot come." So the Jews said, "Will He kill Himself, because He says, 'Where I go you cannot come'?" And He said to them, "You are from beneath; I am from above. You are of this world; I am not of this world. Therefore I said to you that you will

die in your sins; for if you do not believe that I am He, you will die in your sins."

See the underlined passage… ***"for if you do not believe that I am He, you will die in your sins."*** Can you see it yet? Let me restate this in my own words…

"I am leaving, but instead of coming with Me, you will die in your sins. That is unless you believe in Me, you will die in your sins."

Again…

"I am going somewhere you cannot go, because you do not believe in Me. Instead of going with me, you will die in your sins."

Still don't see it? Let's look a few verses past this and see if it becomes clear. ***John 8:28-29...***

Then Jesus said to them, "When you lift up the Son of Man, then you will know that I am He, and that I do nothing of Myself; but as My Father taught Me, I speak these things. And He who sent Me is with Me. The Father has not left Me alone, for I always do those things that please Him."

"***When you lift up the Son of Man, then you will know that I am He***" Jesus says here that what He means will become clear when He is lifted up. What does He mean by "lifted up"? He is referring to His death on the cross. He is saying that when you lift Me up on the cross, the meanings of these things will become evident.

So again…

"I am getting ready to leave" (die on the cross)

"You cannot go with Me" (this was His job to do alone)

"Instead, you will die in your sins" (Because they did not believe)

Again…

"I am going to die on the cross and you are going to die in your sins"

You see, it is not a matter of whether or not they would perish as a result of their disbelief, but rather a "when" and "how" matter.

"When" they die is at the cross when He left them, or when He died.

"How" they died is "in their sins".

When Jesus died, whoever did not believe in Him died in their sins, which not so coincidentally was everyone.

Christians today say they believe, but like we read above, so did the disciples, but Jesus said they didn't. Besides, today is different than their day, because the requirement of belief was to escape dying in their sins when He left at the cross. He was not talking about believing in Him after He did His work. He was saying, "Believe in Me or when I die, you will die in your sins."

Let's look at John 3:16 again.

For God so loved the world that He gave His only begotten Son, that whoever believes in Him should not perish but have everlasting life.

This statement comes from Jesus near the beginning of His ministry. As time moves forward He slowly reveals that they cannot and do not believe. So that means that no one could receive eternal life through belief. So if anyone is to obtain eternal life it would have to come by another means.

As it turns out, this is the entire point of the matter!

Jesus disqualified everyone through His fierce application of an already fierce and unmerciful law.

He made it so that no one could qualify to receive eternal life on their own. He, in essence, took away the hope of eternal life from all of mankind.

Think about that for a moment. He came, teaching people who were already under the law that the law in its fullness, including the new requirement of belief, was the only way to get into heaven. When the end came, no one qualified through the work of the law, so everyone died in their sins.

The Big Switch

So now that Jesus has died, and those who remain here (which was everyone else except for Him) died in their sins, what way is left for inheriting eternal life?

Again, this is the point we are trying to make. Jesus made it so that He was the only one that could redeem mankind from their sins.

He listed the qualifications for earning eternal life so that mankind would know beyond the shadow of a doubt that earning eternal life is impossible.

This brings us to the most climactic point in time in all of human history.

When the time came for those without sin to be granted

eternal life and for those with sin to be punished Jesus stepped in and made what we call the "Big Switch". That is when He took the sin of mankind upon Himself and for the first time since the Garden of Eden, mankind was sinless.

While Jesus carried our sin, the punishment came and the only one deserving of punishment at that time was the sin bearer.

He knew the wrath was coming.

He knew the punishment was coming.

He knew that the peoples of earth, past, present and future, were about to receive the guilty verdict and face wrath and death.

Then in that moment and with all love and compassion, He stepped in and switched places with us and took all of the wrath, the punishment, and the guilt for us.

This is why God wouldn't allow someone the ability to believe.

If they had believed then He would have been forced to "heal" them, or make them whole.

The "Big Switch" wouldn't work if anyone had qualified on their own. So the fact that no one believed was a gift to ALL. Our "imperfections" as a race are indeed a gift. We are made "imperfect" so that He could show His mercy upon us.

When Jesus Died, ALL Died!!!

Though we feel that the words and actions of Christ prove this to be the case, we would like to examine other places in the New Testament that support our claims. Look what Paul says in (MKJV) ***Romans 11:32...***

For God has shut up all in unbelief, so that He might show mercy to all.

If you read all of Romans 11, you will find that Paul is talking about the gift of redemption. He is saying that the Gentiles (non-Jews) didn't believe in God before Jesus came. The Jews were His chosen people, but because they didn't believe in Jesus, their Savior, God's promise also passed to the Gentiles as well. Therefore it was beneficial for ALL that NONE believed.

Look here in ***2Corinthians 5:14...***

For the love of Christ compels us, because we judge thus: that if One died for all, then all died;

It seems that Paul came to the same conclusion. If one man, Jesus, died in place of mankind, then we, ALL of mankind, died as well.

It is simple mathematics. If J (Jesus) represents X (every man), then J=X, and whatever happens to J, also happens to X, right? Jesus (J) represented every man (X) at the cross. When He died, everything He represented died also.

Right now, we are talking about people, but later, we will be talking about what else Jesus represented that died when He died.

So why would it be beneficial for everyone to die when He died?

God's scales are honest. He is loving and merciful, but He is also just.

(This argument is often used against us in debates, but we believe that this fact lends to our argument quite well.)

He is just and so demands Justice.

If there is a crime, there should be a penalty, and that penalty should equal the crime, right? An eye for an eye, a tooth for a tooth…

So how is Justice served if no man is punished for their sins? It is simple. Jesus (J) represented every man (X) at the cross.

When J died, X died.

The Bible tells us, and most if not all CAM members agree, that when Jesus died on the cross He took upon Himself the sins of the world.

If J=X, and S represents sin, then JS=XS. Jesus, with the sins of the world upon Him, is equal to every man with every single sin ever committed.

If this is true, then when Jesus was punished by death for the sins of the world, His punishment was also applied to man and man died too.

You see, Jesus never physically sinned, yet He was punished.

We were not punished although we physically sinned.

Jesus was our representative.

Was Jesus Sacrifice Enough??

If I told you that I just changed the oil in my car, it really wouldn't matter if you believed me or not. I either did or I didn't and your belief or acceptance of this will not change the outcome.

It is the same with Jesus.

The Bible says that He saved the World and your belief or acceptance or lack of either has no bearing on whether or not this is really the case.

I am aware that some gifts require acceptance, but hopefully by the end of this chapter you will see that not all gifts require acceptance.

In fact, some gifts cannot be turned down, no matter what!!

The bigger question I finally found myself asking is "Did God accept Christ's sacrifice?"

Let's read this account in Isaiah 53. This was written hundreds of years before Jesus lived, and yet it very accurately describes the plan that was fulfilled in Christ… ***Isaiah 53…***

Who has believed our report? And to whom has the arm of the LORD been revealed? For He shall grow up before Him as a tender plant, And as a root out of dry ground. He has no form or comeliness; And when we see Him, There is no beauty that we should desire Him. He is despised and rejected by men, A Man of sorrows and acquainted with grief. And we hid, as it were, our faces from Him; He was despised, and we did not esteem Him. Surely He has borne our griefs And carried our sorrows; Yet we esteemed Him stricken, Smitten by God, and afflicted. But He was wounded for our transgressions, He was bruised for our iniquities; The chastisement for our peace was upon Him, And by His stripes we are healed. All we like sheep have gone astray; We have turned, every one, to his own way; And the LORD has laid on Him the iniquity of us all. He was

oppressed and He was afflicted, Yet He opened not His mouth; He was led as a lamb to the slaughter, And as a sheep before its shearers is silent, So He opened not His mouth. He was taken from prison and from judgment, And who will declare His generation? For He was cut off from the land of the living; For the transgressions of My people He was stricken. And they made His grave with the wicked— But with the rich at His death, Because He had done no violence, Nor was any deceit in His mouth. Yet it pleased the LORD to bruise Him; He has put Him to grief. When You make His soul an offering for sin, He shall see His seed, He shall prolong His days, And the pleasure of the LORD shall prosper in His hand. He shall see the labor of His soul, and be satisfied. By His knowledge My righteous Servant shall justify many, For He shall bear their iniquities. Therefore I will divide Him a portion with the great, And He shall divide the spoil with the strong, Because He poured out His soul unto death, And He was numbered with the transgressors, And He bore the sin of many, And made intercession for the transgressors.

Jesus sacrifice satisfied God!!

Is that not enough?

Jesus took His blood to the Father and offered it for the forgiveness of ALL!!

God has accepted His payment of our debt!!

Does He now demand payment from me?

Where is Justice if Jesus represents every man (every non-believing man at that), and was punished, but then God still requires punishment for sins committed by unbelieving men?

Did Jesus die for believers, or unbelievers?

Look at ***Romans 5:6-8...***

For when we were still without strength, in due time Christ died for the ungodly. For scarcely for a righteous man will one die; yet perhaps for a good man someone would even dare to die. But God demonstrates His own love toward us, in that while we were still sinners, Christ died for us.

Christ died for sinners. Christians call themselves "believers" (although no one "truly" believed before, not even the disciples), and they say that they are no longer sinners because of their belief. But Paul says that Jesus died for the sinners. Look at verse ***10...***

For if when we were enemies we were reconciled to God through the death of His Son, much more, having been reconciled, we shall be saved by His life.

Paul, again, says that we were reconciled to God ***when we were His enemies***.

He did not say that the day we became God's friend He was friendly back and therefore reconciled our relationship.

NO, God made the first move.

We were taught that when we believe, then we are reconciled to God, but what we see here is reconciliation on God's part first, then if believing happens the friendship is realized.

He forgave us long before we ever knew Him. He is not waiting on our move. He desires for us to know of His Love and Mercy, but the Love and Mercy is there whether or not we ever acknowledge it.

I had a friend just the other day say that Heaven is like a scenario she was going through. She let some friends stay in her home for a little while and apparently the children were very disrespectful. Because of this disrespect, she has not allowed these people to return to her home. I certainly do not blame her for this. I wouldn't let them stay in my home either.

But God is different. He treats His enemies better than they treat Him, or they deserve to be treated.

Just like Paul says here in Romans 5, no one wants to die, but for a good person or a friend, one might be willing to do so. What makes Jesus better than any of us is His willingness to die for those who hate Him. The very people that punched Him in the face and spit in His eyes, and whipped Him over and over were the same people that He represented when He died.

Our Representative

Let's look for more evidence of Jesus representing every man at the cross… Hebrews 2:9...

But we see Jesus, who was made a little lower than the angels, for the suffering of death crowned with glory and honor, that He, by the grace of God, might taste death for everyone.

Here again, Paul says Jesus tasted death for ALL. So, Christ died for ALL, and represented ALL at His death.

How does that effect our eternity?

Like we stated earlier, whatever happens to Christ happens to man because He represented ALL men.

Jesus died on the cross and we died also.

Three and a half days later He is discovered to be alive again.

So, if J=X, then ALL of mankind, who died with Christ, were given new life when Christ was also given new life at His resurrection. ***Ephesians 2:4-6...***

But God, who is rich in mercy, because of His great love with which He loved us, even when we were dead in trespasses, made us alive together with Christ (by grace you have been saved), and raised us up together, and made us sit together in the heavenly places in Christ Jesus,

Here Paul says that when we were dead in our sins God made us alive together with Christ. We just read that Jesus said that when He dies on the cross, man would die in their sins. Look how this verse reads in the NLT...

But God is so rich in mercy, that even while we were dead because of our sins, he gave us life when he raised Christ from the dead, (It is only by God's special favor that you have been saved!) For he has raised us from the dead along with Christ, and we are seated with him in the heavenly realms- all because we are one with Christ Jesus.

You see, Jesus said in John 8 that He was going to leave (at the cross). Instead of going with Him, He told them that they would die in their sins because of their unbelief. Here, Paul says that while we were dead in our sins (when Jesus was dead), God made us ALIVE when He made Christ come to Life at His resurrection!! We were given new life when Christ was raised, not after we said a prayer and confessed to believe it.

Seemingly Contradictory…

So what do we do about the Bible verses that seem to contradict our claim?

Just like what we hope you do when you find a verse that seems to contradict what you think is true, we have chosen to dive into the passage in question, rather than run from it.

One of the first verses to come up in our debates, (after John 3:16 of course), is Romans 10:9. We mentioned this in the beginning of this chapter because it does seem to contradict our view… that is until you look at it a little closer. ***Romans 10:9…***

> ***that if you confess with your mouth the Lord Jesus and believe in your heart that God has raised Him from the dead, you will be saved.***

After spending years in CAM believing churches, I was very familiar with the word "saved". We were taught that one is "saved" from Hell when they say the sinner's prayer, (which we will be looking into very closely in chapter 3). As you know by now, we believe that ALL were saved from the penalties of sin when Jesus died and rose again. So what does Paul mean by "saved" here in Romans 10:9? The answer, like ALL the answers, will only appear during close examination. Let's look at a few other verses leading up to verse 9. ***Romans 10:1…***

> ***Brethren, my heart's desire and prayer to God for Israel is that they may be saved.***

There is that word "saved" again. Paul says here that it is his wish that Israel would be saved, but saved from what? ***verse***

2...

For I bear them witness that they have a zeal for God, but not according to knowledge.

He says that Israel has a zeal for God, but their knowledge is limited. What knowledge do they lack?

For they being ignorant of God's righteousness, and seeking to establish their own righteousness, have not submitted to the righteousness of God.

He says they lack knowledge of God’s righteousness.

He didn’t say that they were having trouble conforming to a certain standard. He said their problem was their lack of knowledge.

You see, the Jews were still trying to follow the Law of Moses, which like we said earlier is impossible. Paul has been teaching all through this letter to the Romans about the Law and the New Righteousness that is apart from the Law (Romans 3:21). Here in chapter 10, he is simply stating that he desires for his Jewish people to come to this knowledge.

Why?

It is because he is talking about salvation from the Law. ***Romans 10:4...***

For Christ is the end of the law for righteousness to everyone who believes.

In other words, if you believe in Christ, your need to follow the law in order to obtain righteousness is eliminated.

You are saved from the miserably impossible task of

following the law. It is so simple. Paul is saying in Romans 10:9 that if you believe in your heart and confess with your mouth that Jesus is the Savior, then you will realize that He gave you your right standing with God and you are required to do nothing to obtain it.

The Jews rejected Christ, therefore they did not have the knowledge that Jesus had already obtained their eternal life for them, therefore they were still trying to obtain a right standing with God on their own, by following the Law.

You cannot find life (real, true abundant life) by trying to conform to an impossible standard and attempting to impress God with your feeble efforts. This path will only lead to misery and destruction. Many have tried, and ALL have failed in their attempt to enter God's kingdom by this gate.

There is a gate however that leads to life, and that is what Paul was hoping that his people would discover. This is also the point of the passages found in Acts 10:43 and Romans 1:16. Paul is simply noting the benefits of believing and accepting what Christ has done for us. He is not saying that your unbelief nullifies the work He did. This same thought is confirmed again in ***1Timothy 4:9-10...***

This is a faithful saying and worthy of all acceptance. For to this end we both labor and suffer reproach, because we trust in the living God, who is the Savior of <u>all men</u>, especially of those who believe.

Jesus "saved" the World, but obviously not everyone believes that or even has any knowledge of the fact.

Look at this passage where Paul describes a ministry of death versus Christ's ministry that is of Life. ***2Corinthians 3:3-17...***

clearly you are an epistle of Christ, ministered by

us, written not with ink but by the Spirit of the living God, not on tablets of stone but on tablets of flesh, that is, of the heart. And we have such trust through Christ toward God. Not that we are sufficient of ourselves to think of anything as being from ourselves, but our sufficiency is from God, who also made us sufficient as ministers of the new covenant, not of the letter but of the Spirit; for the letter kills, but the Spirit gives life. But if the ministry of death, written and engraved on stones, was glorious, so that the children of Israel could not look steadily at the face of Moses because of the glory of his countenance, which glory was passing away, how will the ministry of the Spirit not be more glorious? For if the ministry of condemnation had glory, the ministry of righteousness exceeds much more in glory. For even what was made glorious had no glory in this respect, because of the glory that excels. For if what is passing away was glorious, what remains is much more glorious. Therefore, since we have such hope, we use great boldness of speech—unlike Moses, who put a veil over his face so that the children of Israel could not look steadily at the end of what was passing away. But their minds were blinded. For until this day the same veil remains unlifted in the reading of the Old Testament, because the veil is taken away in Christ. But even to this day, when Moses is read, a veil lies on their heart. Nevertheless when one turns to the Lord, the veil is taken away. Now the Lord is the Spirit; and where the Spirit of the Lord is, there is liberty.

There is a lot to consider in the above passage.

First of all, Paul clearly describes the 10 commandments and the Law when he says that the New Covenant is not like the one written on stone tablets. He says that that covenant is Moses' ministry of DEATH and Condemnation!!! He also says that when we look to Moses' covenant for our righteousness, we have a veil on our hearts.

This is exactly what he was talking about in Romans 10. Paul's people, the Jews, were looking to Moses for their right standing with God. This caused them to miss the New Covenant that Jesus acquired for us. Not that they would not receive the benefits upon their death, but they surely would not be enjoying the knowledge that Jesus sacrifice has made us free from the Law.

The New Covenant is Life, while the Old Covenant (which many still attempt to follow) is Death and destruction.

Jesus mentions these two paths in a parable. ***Matthew 7:13-14...***

"Enter by the narrow gate; for wide is the gate and broad is the way that leads to destruction, and there are many who go in by it. Because narrow is the gate and difficult is the way which leads to life, and there are few who find it.

The first time I was shown this passage, I was told that Jesus was saying that "*sinners have it easy, and so they go in through the wide gate, but we Christians must take the difficult, narrow path that leads to life*". That is probably what most people see when they read this passage, but remember, Jesus taught in parables that are mysterious.

If you find the answer to the riddle in the first 10 seconds of reading it you are either really smart or you were only seeing what appears on the surface.

In this passage, it is very easy to interpret Jesus teaching as a warning to follow the Law to receive life, but like ALL of His parables, there is a degree of hindsight that must be considered when searching for the answers. Jesus was teaching in parables about the Kingdom of God, but there were parts of the plan that were hidden from them at the present time. It isn't until after the events of the cross and resurrection that we can look back and see what He meant by those things. Obviously He is teaching about two paths, one leading to life and one to destruction. Paul continues this theme in many of his writings, comparing the path of Moses' Law that leads to death and the path to Life that Jesus blazed for us.

Surely you can see that many have found the wide path the CAM member follows and, with all of the rules and regulations, this path leads to their destruction. Very few have ever realized that Jesus did it all for you and you don't even have to try.

God is pleased with you, even on your worst days. Knowing this is uncommon and is the key to having Life!!!

<u>The Misleading "IF"</u>

Look at this verse that we mentioned in the beginning of this chapter. It is quite popular to CAM teachers… ***2Corinthians 5:17…***

> ***Therefore, <u>if</u> anyone is in Christ, he is a new creation; old things have passed away; behold, all things have become new.***

In all my years in church, I heard this one verse quoted by itself hundreds of times. It is almost always used to explain the CAM theory that when an individual makes the good decision to accept Christ, then and only then do they become a new creature or are given new life. The use of "if" and "anyone" in this passage seems to support this claim, but when read with the verses before it, look what happens…

2Corinthians 5:14-21...

For the love of Christ compels us, because we judge thus: that if One died for all, then all died; and He died for all, that those who live should live no longer for themselves, but for Him who died for them and rose again. Therefore, from now on, we regard no one according to the flesh. Even though we have known Christ according to the flesh, yet now we know Him thus no longer. Therefore, if anyone is in Christ, he is a new creation; old things have passed away; behold, all things have become new. Now all things are of God, who has reconciled us to Himself through Jesus Christ, and has given us the ministry of reconciliation, that is, that God was in Christ reconciling the world to Himself, not imputing their trespasses to them, and has committed to us the word of reconciliation. Now then, we are ambassadors for Christ, as though God were pleading through us: we implore you on Christ's behalf, be reconciled to God. For He made Him who knew no sin to be sin for us, that we might become the righteousness of God in Him.

Go ahead and read this passage again, slowly and many times.

You will find that Paul is saying that because Jesus died for ALL, then ALL died, and if anyone is in Christ, he is made new.

There are two "if"s underlined in the passage. Neither of them is there to signify doubt or a chance that it will or did not happen. These are "If/Then" statements. Paul is simply saying that IF Christ died for ALL, (and we know He did) - THEN ALL died in Christ, and ALL are made alive as New Creatures.

Look at the end of this passage again. It says "***For He has made Him who knew no sin, to be sin for us, that we might become the righteousness of God in Him.".***

The word "might" in this sentence has also been used by CAM teachers to suggest that this means this "might" not happen. But if you read it slowly, it soon becomes obvious that this "might" is used to show intention just like the IF/THEN statements.

Just as I say, "I am going to town that I might get some milk". I am not saying that I think this might not happen. I know there will be milk at the store. I know I have enough money in my pocket to buy it. I am merely saying that the purpose of my trip is to get milk.

In this passage, Paul is merely stating that the purpose of God making Jesus, the one who did not sin to be sin for us, or in our place, was so that we would become the righteousness of God in Him.

When Jesus represented us on the cross, the sins of the world were added to Him and the punishment He endured as the result was credited to us as a paid debt, making us righteous.

Reading the verse again, ***2Corinthians 5:17...***

> ***Therefore, if anyone is in Christ, he is a new creation; old things have passed away; behold, all things have become new.***

The "Old things" that passed away are the Law and now everything has been made New in the light of the New Covenant. We will be talking more about New and Old things throughout this book, but one of my favorite Old/New comparisons will come in Chapter 4 where we will show you something Old that was made New in the book of

Revelations.

Until then, let's keep going. ***Romans 6:4-11...***

Therefore we were buried with Him through baptism into death, that just as Christ was raised from the dead by the glory of the Father, even so we also should walk in newness of life. For if we have been united together in the likeness of His death, certainly we also shall be in the likeness of His resurrection, knowing this, that our old man was crucified with Him, that the body of sin might be done away with, that we should no longer be slaves of sin. For he who has died has been freed from sin. Now if we died with Christ, we believe that we shall also live with Him, knowing that Christ, having been raised from the dead, dies no more. Death no longer has dominion over Him. For the death that He died, He died to sin once for all; but the life that He lives, He lives to God. Likewise you also, reckon yourselves to be dead indeed to sin, but alive to God in Christ Jesus our Lord.

This passage is much like the one we just read from 2Corinthians 5. Paul is again assuring us that when Jesus died at the cross, ALL of us died. We were symbolically buried with Him into death and when He rose from the dead, we were given New Life.

Look closely at verse ***6... "knowing this, that our old man was crucified with Him, that the body of sin might be done away with..."***

When something is "done away with", it is discarded.

When Jesus was on the cross, the sins of the entire world were on Him. His body died and therefore, the "body" of sin was done away with.

When Jesus rose again, He had a glorified body because He was made new.

In chapter 6, we will show you more symbolic proof of how the "body of sin" has been discarded and destroyed by fire in one of the most controversial passages of the Bible.

Obvious Tampering…

Many times during our debates, we will argue the point that belief is a "pre-cross" issue. In defense, we are often presented with this passage found in ***Mark 16:15-16...***

> ***And He said to them, "Go into all the world and preach the gospel to every creature. He who believes and is baptized will be saved; but he who does not believe will be condemned.***

I will admit that for a little while, early in my studies, this passage had me stumped. It was the only one that I couldn't hurdle. Like all the others, we chose to confront the passage and see if there was perhaps something more to it than what we were seeing. Because I do a lot of studying on my computer Bible, I do not have footnotes to read. I do however keep a few hardcopies of the book around. It just so happens that while I was staring at this passage, I thought I might see what the footnotes in my paper copy said. I also urge you to find a copy of the Bible with footnotes, or search Mark 16:9-20 on the internet. You will find, as I did, that this passage was not found in the oldest of manuscripts, but appears to be added by somebody. How's is that for trusting the "Bible"? You see, as we said before, when you read any English copy of the Bible, you are not reading what the authors penned, but rather what a group of translators thought it meant. If you could trust any one of the English Bibles, which would it be? You cannot say ALL of them, because there are obvious differences in them all. Without comparing every passage to the originals, you can't really take any of it at face value. You must be willing to dig deeper to find the answers.

The Rich Man

Belief in Christ, for the purpose of obtaining eternal life, is a pre-cross issue. No one, including Jesus' own disciples, could do it. Yet today we have millions of CAM members now saying, as the disciples did then, that they believe and that their belief qualifies them.

Belief in Christ is very valuable as it can set your mind free from the thinking that you are at odds with God, but thinking that your belief is what qualifies you for the prize of eternal life is a legalistic view that is faulty.

The disciples claimed often that their belief was real and sufficient. Every time, Christ returned their statements with His own view that their faith was not enough to qualify them.

Did they believe He existed?

Of course, they physically touched Him.

Was it enough?

Jesus said that it was not.

Do you believe in Jesus?

I hope so, as I know what impact this belief has had on my life, but is it enough to qualify you?

Jesus dealt with this issue in the story of the Rich man and Lazarus found in ***Luke 16:19-31...***

"There was a certain rich man who was clothed in purple and fine linen and fared sumptuously every day. But there was a certain beggar named Lazarus, full of sores, who was laid at his gate, desiring to be fed with the crumbs which fell from the rich man's table. Moreover the dogs came and licked his sores. So it was that the beggar died, and was carried by the angels to Abraham's bosom. The rich man also died and was buried. And being in torments in Hades, he lifted up his eyes and saw Abraham afar off, and Lazarus in his bosom. "Then he cried and said, 'Father Abraham, have mercy on me, and send Lazarus that he may dip the tip of his finger in water and cool my tongue; for I am tormented in this flame.' But Abraham said, 'Son, remember that in your lifetime you received your good things, and likewise Lazarus evil things; but now he is comforted and you are tormented. And besides all this, between us and you there is a great gulf fixed, so that those who want to pass from here to you cannot, nor can those from there pass to us.' "Then he said, 'I beg you therefore, father, that you would send him to my father's house, for I have five brothers, that he may testify to them, lest they also come to this place of torment.' Abraham said to him, 'They have Moses and the prophets; let them hear them.' And he said, 'No, father Abraham; but if one goes to them from the dead, they will repent.' But he said to him, 'If they do not hear Moses and the prophets, neither will they be persuaded though one rise from the dead.' "

There are many wonderful discoveries in the parable of the rich man and Lazarus, but the punch line remains that even if someone is raised from the dead people will still not be persuaded, which would happen if they truly believed. We may believe, but not enough to qualify us. Instead, He qualified for us. He did this so that it would be by His love and mercy alone that we are together with Him.

What if we are wrong?

CAM members have often tried to scare us with questions like "What if you are wrong?"

The reason they ask this is because they think that believing in Jesus is the only way to get to heaven.

They think this because of many different passages in the Bible including this one, ***John 14:6...***

Jesus said to him, "I am the way, the truth, and the life. No one comes to the Father except through Me.

My question is this, do you think that people will not believe in Jesus based on the message that Jesus died for your sins whether you believe it or not?

Quite the contrary.

I have had several atheists tell me that the reason they believe that there is no God is because of the hypocrisy and horrible message of the CAM. They have also told me that if such a God existed that was good to everyone, even if they weren't good back, then they would be interested in knowing this God. The sad thing is that this is not the God that the CAM talks about.

The truth is simple... Everyone will find Heaven to be their home, but not because they believed or did what they were supposed to do, but simply because Jesus did what He was supposed to do. Jesus is the way. Your belief in Him is irrelevant.

Do You Now Believe???

As we mentioned in the beginning of this chapter, CAM members will tell you that although Jesus paid your debt, it is still your responsibility to "accept" this free gift he has given. They say it is like a car that, although it has been given to you, you have to pick up the keys and drive it for it to be of any use to you. The way this is said sounds logical and therefore is easily accepted as the truth.

What we would like to suggest now is that the Gift of God is not like a car. The word "car" in the English language is a noun. A noun is a thing or an idea. It can be held or perceived. It can also be destroyed.

Jesus gift to mankind is a verb or an action.

Have you ever tried to stop an action after it has already happened?

That is why the plan was so mysterious. That is why Jesus could not tell them the whole story. If He made it clear to them that His death on the cross was the plan, they would not have understood and they would have stopped it from happening.

The Good News is that they DID NOT understand and therefore Jesus was able to do His work. Jesus took the sins of the World to the cross and your belief or lack of does not affect the outcome of His action.

What is done is done and your acceptance of it is irrelevant when it comes to its effect.

Here is further proof… ***Romans 3:3-4…***

> ***For what if some did not believe? Will their unbelief make the faithfulness of God without effect? Certainly not! Indeed, let God be true but every man a liar. As it is written: "THAT YOU MAY BE JUSTIFIED IN YOUR WORDS, AND MAY OVERCOME WHEN YOU ARE JUDGED."***

Again in ***2Timothy 2:13…***

If we are faithless, He remains faithful; He cannot deny Himself.

In these two passages, Paul confirms that our belief has nothing to do with the eternal outcome of the situation. Jesus' gift is not like a car. Forget the car!!! Not ALL gifts require your acceptance. Imagine if a bear were chasing you with an obvious intent on eating you for dinner. If I shoot the bear, would that not be a gift? Does this gift require your acceptance? No way. I chose to shoot the bear. You might even have wished to be eaten, but your will in this instance does not matter. The action is done and whether you believe or not or appreciate it or not, it is finished. God's gift is irrevocable.

Jesus is the Messiah that was sent to save us from the penalties of our sin. He did it whether you believe He did or not.

He didn't get any big "high fives" or fireworks or standing ovations like heroes we often think about. Usually a hero's hour of glory is very obvious, but on this day, hanging from a cross, naked, bleeding, and weak, this hero saved the world in The Hour We Least Expected.

I hope you believe it.

The Hour We Least Expected

Chapter 3

Is It Your Choice?

In chapter 2, we discussed the Currently Accepted Message (CAM) view of the issue of belief. According to the CAM, not only is our eternal security based upon our belief in Jesus Christ, but it is also required that we make a conscious choice to "make" Him our Lord and Savior.

The two ideas, belief and choice, go hand in hand and although they are so very similar, we have decided to look at God's plan for our salvation from the penalties of sin from the angle of it being our choice.

Is it our choice to "make" Jesus Lord or is He Lord already? Is it our choice to "make" Jesus our Savior, or is He the Savior of the whole world and not by anyone's choice but His? Do we pick Him or does He pick us? If it is our choice, how do we make it? What do we need to do to prove that we have made the choice? If He picks us then does He pick all of us, part of us, or none of us?

The CAM Theory

It is the view of the CAM that we must choose our final

destination. They say that God will not "force" His love on us. It is up to us to "accept" His love for us and prove our acceptance of Him by loving Him back.

According to the CAM, if we do not make the choice to "make" Jesus our personal Lord and Savior, then by default, we have made "Hell" our home for eternity.

In other words, God wants us to live with Him in Heaven forever, but sin is not allowed in Heaven. Therefore, if we do not accept Jesus sacrifice for our sins and let Him wash our guilt away, then we have chosen the alternative.

Here are a couple of the most common Bible passages that are used to make these suggestions ***John 14:6, John 3:3 respectively...***

Jesus said to him, "I am the way, the truth, and the life. No one comes to the Father except through Me.

Jesus answered and said to him, "Most assuredly, I say to you, unless one is born again, he cannot see the kingdom of God."

Is Jesus saying here in these two instances that we have a choice to make?

The CAM says so.

We are going to look even further into what CAM members believe and what process they say we must go through to comply with these statements made by Jesus and then we are going to show you why we disagree as we shed some light on the intentions of these statements that Jesus has made in these two verses and more.

Loopholes

John 14:6...

Jesus said to him, "I am the way, the truth, and the life. No one comes to the Father except through Me.

Ask any CAM leader what you must do to get to Heaven, and most likely they will tell you that you must believe in Jesus.

Then ask them what happens to babies when they die.

They will most likely tell you that God has set an age of accountability and if a person has not yet reached that age, then they are not held accountable for making this decision to believe.

Then ask them what happens to people that have never heard of Jesus.

They will most likely tell you that it would not be fair for such people to be held accountable because of their ignorance of the Savior.

Then ask them what happened to the handicapped that are unable to make the decision and you will get a similar answer.

My question is this…

If most people reject Christ when given the opportunity to do so, why are we telling everyone about Him?

And why are we allowing our children to grow up?

If most adults are going to Hell once they find out about Jesus, then wouldn't we be doing them an eternal favor by keeping them unaccountable?

The truth is simple…

Jesus' mission was to save the World. The Good News is that He pulled it off without a hitch and without our help. He is the Truth and as we stated before. Truth is no less true due to a lack of supporters.

Where does the CAM Get Its Information?

As we said, the CAM believes that we all have a personal choice to make. According to them, there is a process that one must go through before they can be called "saved".

Copied below is the famous Romans Road that we were taught in church to use as a tool to get someone "saved" from the penalties of sin. You can find this online by searching "Romans Road" or simply ask any CAM teacher and they can probably quote it for you.

It is called "Romans Road" because of the many verses they have linked together that are all taken from the letter Paul wrote to the church in Rome. Here are the verses and how they are explained by the CAM and then in *italics*, what action they say you must take to comply with the corresponding verse...

Romans 3:23 "For all have sinned and fall short of the glory of God."
We all have sin in our hearts. We all were born with sin. We were born under the power of sin's control.
- Admit that you are a sinner.
Romans 6:23a "...The wages of sin is death..."
Sin has an ending. It results in death. We all face physical death, which is a result of sin. But a worse death is spiritual death that alienates us from God, and will last for all eternity. The Bible teaches that there is a place called the Lake of Fire where lost people will be in torment forever. It is the place where people who are spiritually dead will remain.
- Understand that you deserve death for your sin.
Romans 6:23b "...but the gift of God is eternal life in Christ Jesus our Lord."
Salvation is a free gift from God to you! You can't earn this gift, but you must reach out and receive it.
- Ask God to forgive you and save you.

Romans 5:8, "But God demonstrates His own love toward us, in that while we were still sinners, Christ died for us."
When Jesus died on the cross He paid sin's penalty. He paid the price for all sin, and when He took all the sins of the world on Himself on the cross, He bought us out of slavery to sin and death! The only condition is that we believe in Him and what He has done for us, understanding that we are now joined with Him, and that He is our life. He did all this because He loved us and gave Himself for us!
- Give your life to God... His love poured out in Jesus on the cross is your only hope to have forgiveness and change. His love bought you out of being a slave to sin. His love is what saves you -- not religion, or church membership. God loves you!
Romans 10:13 "For "WHOEVER CALLS ON THE NAME OF THE LORD SHALL BE SAVED."
- Call out to God in the name of Jesus!
Romans 10:9,10 that if you confess with your mouth the Lord Jesus and believe in your heart that God has raised Him from the dead, you will be saved. For with the heart one believes unto righteousness, and with the mouth confession is made unto salvation.
- If you know that God is knocking on your heart's door,
ask Him to come into your heart.

Along with this process of "accepting" Jesus, there is a special prayer that basically signifies your choice. They call it the "Sinners Prayer".

Being that I was a former CAM member, I have said the Sinners Prayer with hundreds of individuals, each time with a feeling of relief that they would now be included in God's family and not tossed out with the sinners.

As we told you in the introduction of this book, we believed these things and we acted upon our beliefs.

It Seems to Make Sense…

The first time I was shown the Romans Road, it made perfect sense. Every verse that is listed seems to say exactly what they taught me that it meant. It wasn't until several years ago that I even thought to question the whole idea and see for myself what these passages actually mean.

Before we dive in to the specifics of this plan or process, let's talk about a few points of logic that we would like you to consider.

First of all, why is this plan not clearly spelled out by Paul in Romans?

Of course CAM members would like to say that it is and they have merely simplified it, but really?

Why didn't Paul put this process in the very first chapter and call it "The Most Important Thing You Will Ever Read in Your Life!!!"?

If this process is God's perfect plan for your salvation, why did He prompt Paul with so much "filler" in his letters?

Search the whole Bible, and you will not find one single place where this plan is clearly spelled out.

You will see very soon that the way this Romans Road has been put together is very much like editing a recorded interview in such a way as to make the interviewee say whatever you want him to say. Combine this edited video with a news reporter stating these things as facts and you will have everyone believing whatever you want them to. The power of suggestion by revered individuals, combined with faulty information can and has caused masses of people to believe lies regarding any situation. Our only hope is that before you make up your mind regarding any subject, you will take the time to research more and not just believe the first story you are told.

The First Step on the Romans Road…

We found it to be extremely ironic that the very first step in the Romans Road would provide us such a strong piece of evidence that so clearly states our claim.

Romans 3:23 is the verse that we were taught to use as the first step in showing someone that they were flawed and that they needed a Savior. ***Romans 3:23...***

> ***for all have sinned and fall short of the glory of God,***

What do you notice about this sentence?

The first thing you should notice is that it is not a sentence at all. It starts with a small letter and ends with a comma. However, in some literature that was dropped off at my house the other day by a local church (and in the Romans Road copied above) the "f" was capitalized and the semi-colon was replaced by a period thus it was rendered as follows:

> *"For all have sinned and come short of the glory of God."*

Wow! It is amazing how a simple change in sentence structure and wording can make a HUGE impact on the meaning or implied meaning of the message?

Like we will mention over and over again, the Bible was not written in chapter and verse. It was written as complete thoughts.

It is not a bunch of bullet points from which you can pull one out of the middle and it can stand as complete truth on its own.

That rings very true in this case. We believe Romans 3 should not be read without considering what the first two chapters are about. After all, this is a letter and was not written in chapters at all.

We will not go through the entire first two chapters, but will give you a quick recap that you can compare to the text yourself and see if we are saying it correctly.

In Romans chapter one, you will find Paul starts writing about a group of people who practice evil things. He mentions some things that they do and how that even though they know that what they do is wrong and is punishable by death, they still do them anyway.

(This is a very popular chapter the CAM often uses to teach against homosexuality because it seems to be described in this chapter. We will not necessarily spend any specific time on this subject of homosexuality, but our stance will become clear as you continue to read.)

Often in debates the other side of the table will take us to this chapter to show how Paul feels about such evil activity.

Again we say that Paul didn't just write chapter one, but you will see that he is using chapter one to set up for chapter two, which is then used to set up for chapter three and what we call "the big but".

In chapter two, Paul starts by saying… ***Romans 2:1...***

Therefore you are inexcusable, O man, whoever you are who judge, for in whatever you judge another

you condemn yourself; for you who judge practice the same things.

He then begins to chew on the people he is writing the letter to, because even though they are Jews, which were previously God's chosen people, and have the Law of Moses, and were supposed to be an example to the rest of the world, they broke the law just like everyone else. Remember, the Law called for total compliance. Even breaking one law, like lying, meant you were just as guilty as a murderer.

He goes on to ask them how they expect to escape God's judgment when they are just as guilty.

(This is also used against us in debates to show that Paul is aware of a future Day of Judgment. We disagree. Paul is talking to people who might think this, but he will soon explain himself after "the big but" of chapter 3. We will be discussing Judgment Day in the next chapter.)

In chapter 3 of Paul's letter to the church in Rome, he continues to discuss the righteousness that comes by obedience to the Law and comes to the conclusion that we, all of mankind, are guilty… ***Romans 3:10-18...***

As it is written: "THERE IS NONE RIGHTEOUS, NO, NOT ONE; THERE IS NONE WHO UNDERSTANDS; THERE IS NONE WHO SEEKS AFTER GOD. THEY HAVE ALL TURNED ASIDE; THEY HAVE TOGETHER BECOME UNPROFITABLE; THERE IS NONE WHO DOES GOOD, NO, NOT ONE." "THEIR THROAT IS AN OPEN TOMB; WITH THEIR TONGUES THEY HAVE PRACTICED DECEIT"; "THE POISON OF ASPS IS UNDER THEIR LIPS"; "WHOSE MOUTH IS FULL OF CURSING AND BITTERNESS." "THEIR FEET ARE SWIFT TO SHED BLOOD;

DESTRUCTION AND MISERY ARE IN THEIR WAYS; AND THE WAY OF PEACE THEY HAVE NOT KNOWN." "THERE IS NO FEAR OF GOD BEFORE THEIR EYES."

He makes it very clear here that no one has what it takes to be declared righteous. ***Romans 3:19-20...***

Now we know that whatever the law says, it says to those who are under the law, that every mouth may be stopped, and all the world may become guilty before God. Therefore by the deeds of the law no flesh will be justified in His sight, for by the law is the knowledge of sin.

You see, in chapter 1, Paul is talking about lawbreakers, and in chapter 2, he comes down on the "pretenders", the ones who acted like they were keeping the Law, and here in chapter 3, he concludes that the Law is impossible to be used as a means of justification.

Lawbreakers and those who try to keep the Law fall in the same category.

No one can keep the Law.

The Law was a tool to put us all in the same position, which is guilty.

Here is the finale of the setup. He has just disqualified everyone from being good enough to be considered right with God, and is now ready for the punch line, or "the big but" as we call it… ***Romans 3:21-22...***

But now the righteousness of God apart from the law is revealed, being witnessed by the Law and the Prophets, even the righteousness of God, through faith

in Jesus Christ, to all and on all who believe. For there is no difference;

This new "righteousness", that has now been revealed, doesn't come by complying with the Law, but came through the faith of Jesus Christ.

It has been given to ALL, and is being experienced by ALL who believe, for there is no difference.

By saying that there is no difference, we must ask "Difference in what?"

You must have at least two things in order to find a difference between them. What are the things here?

Read it very carefully and you will see that two groups of people are being compared here, ALL and ALL who believe.

I know many will argue here and say that this verse says that you must believe to qualify, but read this closely. Paul says that this has been revealed. He doesn't say that a new way to become righteous has been revealed, but that the righteousness itself has been revealed.

You see, in verse 20, he says that the Law, or the Old Covenant, revealed or gave us the knowledge of sin. Sin was always here, but was revealed by the Law.

This righteousness was also always here, but was not revealed until Jesus spelled out the terms of the New Covenant by taking all of the blame and dying in our place.

Look what Paul says here in ***2Timothy 1:9-10...***

who has saved us and called us with a holy calling, not according to our works, but according to

His own purpose and grace which was given to us in Christ Jesus before time began, but has now been revealed by the appearing of our Savior Jesus Christ, who has abolished death and brought life and immortality to light through the gospel,

He says that this grace, which is the new righteousness, was given to us before time began, but was not revealed until Jesus defeated death and brought life and immortality to light through His good work.

So what about our Romans Road? Here was our first stop, but this time in complete sentences… ***Romans 3:21-26(MKJV)…***

But now a righteousness of God has been revealed apart from Law, being witnessed by the Law and the Prophets; even the righteousness of God through the faith of Jesus Christ, toward all and upon all those who believe. For there is no difference, <u>for all have sinned and come short of the glory of God</u>, being justified freely by His grace through the redemption that is in Christ Jesus; whom God has set forth to be a propitiation through faith in His blood, to declare His righteousness through the passing by of the sins that had taken place before, in the forbearance of God; for the display of His righteousness at this time, for Him to be just and, forgiving the one being of the faith of Jesus.

Underlined here is the one verse, Romans 3:23 that is quoted alone in the Romans Road. Now let's break down this one long sentence…

"For there is no difference, <u>for all have sinned and come short of the glory of God</u>, being justified freely by His grace through the redemption that is in Christ Jesus;"

First notice that it starts with “For there is no difference”.

No difference in what?

Look at the sentence above it and all that was discussed in the letter up until now. Paul is saying that whether you are a Jew or Greek, a believer or a doubter, THERE IS NO DIFFERENCE… for ALL have sinned and come short of the glory of God. Paul is merely wrapping up his huge point that this affects us ALL.

Now look at the next segment. Paul says that ALL have sinned, AND are being justified FREELY by His grace. The same ALL that sinned is also justified freely because of the grace that was revealed because of what Jesus did for us. The point of this sentence is not to point out that we are all sinners, but that we are all equal and now justified.

Let’s keep going with this sentence…

whom God has set forth to be a propitiation through faith in His blood,

Again, read this closely.

Paul says that GOD was the one who gave Jesus the instruction to do this and be the propitiation, (propitiate means to win somebody’s favor, in this case God’s) God did this through faith in Jesus blood. God did it. So whose faith is this sentence referring to?

Paul is not saying that we have to have faith in His blood. Not one time in this passage does he mention that you must have faith to receive it. There are instances where Paul mentions our faith, but it is for our own mental benefit to believe, not to qualify us for the prize of eternal life.

Jesus alone, without our help and without our faith, qualified us.

It is the trust in Him that gives us the peace that passes all understanding, but many trust in their ability to make a wise decision, and call it trusting in Jesus. But if you know that Jesus has saved you, whether you asked Him to or not, then there is a peace that comes over you that is like no other.

The rest of this sentence…

to declare His righteousness through the passing by of the sins that had taken place before, in the forbearance of God; for the display of His righteousness at this time, for Him to be just and, forgiving the one being of the faith of Jesus.

This sentence is still about God giving us Jesus. Now read this last part slowly.

Paul says that Jesus declared His righteousness by the passing of the sins that took place before.

You see, because God knew what He was going to do long before Jesus was born on the Earth, He did not punish anyone that died before the coming of the Lord. This is so that Jesus could take upon Himself the punishment for ALL sins committed, not just those before, but after the cross too.

Again, don't read this verse wrong. The end says "***forgiving the one being of the faith of Jesus.***" It means that God, by sending Jesus to the cross, and not punishing anyone before, was displaying His righteousness at this time and His justice, by forgiving those who were a product of the faith that God and Jesus shared and used to accomplish this. We are a product of that faith.

Romans 3:27-28...

Where is boasting then? It is excluded. By what law? Of works? No, but by the law of faith. Therefore we conclude that a man is justified by faith apart from the deeds of the law.

Why would Paul even mention that boasting is excluded if we are wrong? Christians boast all of the time about how superior they are to the rest of the world because they were smart enough to accept Jesus.

Again, what they are really trusting in is their ability to make a good choice. If it is our choice, then boasting is not excluded, because some are in a better standing with God than others.

So as for the first stop along the Romans Road, we find this point "that ALL have sinned and fall short of the glory of God", to only prove our theory that ALL do not qualify on their own, yet ALL are included in the righteousness that is now revealed.

The Second Stop on The Romans Road...

Let's go on to the next stop... ***Romans 6:23...***

For the wages of sin is death, but the gift of God is eternal life in Christ Jesus our Lord.

This is the last verse in this chapter. In order to understand the meaning of this, you must read the entire letter, but at least read the chapter that it was included in. If you read the whole letter, and read it slowly, without any preconceived ideas of what it is supposed to be about, you will find that Paul is saying, in this chapter, that when Jesus was crucified, those whom He represented, (ALL), were crucified with Him.

Remember this verse… ***Matthew 3:11...***

I indeed baptize you with water unto repentance, but He who is coming after me is mightier than I, whose sandals I am not worthy to carry. He will baptize you with the Holy Spirit and fire.

This was John the Baptist words. He baptized with water for the repentance of sins. But He says Jesus was going to baptize us with the Holy Spirit and fire. There is no record in the Bible of Jesus baptizing anyone, so what is John talking about?

Look what Paul says here in ***Romans 6:3-5...***

Or do you not know that as many of us as were baptized into Christ Jesus were baptized into His death? Therefore we were buried with Him through baptism into death, that just as Christ was raised from the dead by the glory of the Father, even so we also should walk in newness of life. For if we have been united together in the likeness of His death, certainly we also shall be in the likeness of His resurrection,

Remember what we covered in chapter 2, and what Paul said in 2Corinthians 5, that if one died for ALL, then ALL died. We died with Him at the cross.

Remember we learned in ***John 8:21-24...***

Then Jesus said to them again, "I am going away, and you will seek Me, and will die in your sin. Where I go you cannot come." So the Jews said, "Will He kill Himself, because He says, 'Where I go you cannot come'?" And He said to them, "You are from beneath; I am from above. You are of this world; I am not of this world. Therefore I said to you that you will

die in your sins; for if you do not believe that I am He, you will die in your sins."

None believed, so ALL died.

Did they have a choice?

Remember ***John 12:38-40...***

that the word of Isaiah the prophet might be fulfilled, which he spoke: "LORD, WHO HAS BELIEVED OUR REPORT? AND TO WHOM HAS THE ARM OF THE LORD BEEN REVEALED?" Therefore they could not believe, because Isaiah said again: "HE HAS BLINDED THEIR EYES AND HARDENED THEIR HEARTS, LEST THEY SHOULD SEE WITH THEIR EYES, LEST THEY SHOULD UNDERSTAND WITH THEIR HEARTS AND TURN, SO THAT I SHOULD HEAL THEM."

The answer is NO; they did not have a choice. It appeared that they did, because Jesus was saying that belief in Him was a requirement, but also remember what we said in the last chapter, that Jesus taught many requirements, including the Law which was impossible for man. So instead of going with Him (when He left, which was at the cross), they died in their sins, but that is the GOOD NEWS!

Ephesians 2:4-7...

But God, who is rich in mercy, because of His great love with which He loved us, even when we were dead in trespasses, made us alive together with Christ (by grace you have been saved), and raised us up together, and made us sit together in the heavenly places in Christ Jesus, that in the ages to come He might show the exceeding riches of His grace in His kindness

toward us in Christ Jesus.

The Good News is that when we were dead in our sins (after Jesus died), God made us alive with Jesus (at His resurrection).

So read this whole chapter in Romans 6. Paul says that we were crucified with Christ, and that makes us justified from sin. This is the fire baptism that John the Baptist was referring to. (We will be learning more about this fire baptism in Chapter 6).

When Christ died, our sins were forgiven and forgotten. They were burned away, forever separated from God, leaving us pure and righteous in God's sight. The righteousness that Jesus maintained on Earth was given to us when He traded places with us at the cross. He traded His perfect, righteous life for the sins of the whole world, and therefore received the wages of sin, which is death as stated here in Romans 6:23, the second stop in the Romans Road.

The Third Stop on the Romans Road…

The third stop on the Romans road is ***Romans 5:8…***

> ***But God demonstrates His own love toward us, in that while we were still sinners, Christ died for us.***

Surely by now, you see that this verse only adds to our theory, but if you're still not there, we really must analyze this whole chapter.

Romans 5 is by far one of the clearest indicators of our common future.

Remember in Romans 1, Paul is talking about all of the wicked people out there that surely will not qualify for eternal life. Then in chapter 2, he turns on his audience by saying that if it is true that these wicked people don't qualify, then it is especially true for them, because they were God's "chosen people" and even though they had the Law to guide them, they still messed up (none of us are perfect as the Law demanded).

In Chapter 3, Paul introduces us to the "big but". He says that ALL deserve punishment and judgment, BUT, God has given us a righteous standing that doesn't require us to follow the Law. He then goes on to say that this was given to us because it was God's plan from the beginning. That is why he says that God did not punish anyone for their sins before the Lord had come. He says that the Faith of Jesus has saved us.

In Chapter 4, you will find that Paul shows that this faith of Jesus mirrors the faith and promise of Abraham that he would become the Father of many nations. Then look at what Paul says in ***Romans 4:14-16...***

For if those who are of the law are heirs, faith is made void and the promise made of no effect, because the law brings about wrath; for where there is no law there is no transgression. Therefore it is of faith that it might be according to grace, so that the promise might be sure to all the seed, not only to those who are of the law, but also to those who are of the faith of Abraham, who is the father of us all

Here he again says that the Law is not what makes us part of God's family, because the Law only brings wrath, but where there is no Law, there is no transgression.

What did he mean by that?

We will be discussing more about the End of the Law later in chapter 4. He says, instead, that it is because of Faith we have been given the Grace (which is the unmerited favor of God, meaning the favor of God that we do not deserve because we did nothing to qualify) Then he says this was so the promise would be made to ALL the seed, not just those under the Law, but to those who were the product of the faith of Abraham which he then says is the Father of us ALL.

Abrahams promise was fulfilled by grafting us ALL into his family. This promise wasn't dependent upon us, but his faith. This promise was made to him. Jesus made good on that promise when He died on the cross. He, by His choice, forgave us and adopted us into the family.

So then we get to chapter 5. ***Romans 5:1-2...***

Therefore, having been justified by faith, we have peace with God through our Lord Jesus Christ, through whom also we have access by faith into this grace in which we stand, and rejoice in hope of the glory of God.

Remember, this letter was not written in chapter and verse form. This next paragraph is built on the paragraphs before it. So when Paul says that we have been justified by faith, you must look at what was said before now to see that this was not our personal faith that justified us.

Jesus died on the cross for my sins whether I believe He did or not. Paul says that because we have been justified, we now have peace with God. Those who were under the Law did not have peace with God, because their eternal life was always in jeopardy before Jesus came. Jesus opened the door with this faith and has given us access to this grace. Now read verses 6-8...

For when we were still without strength, in due time Christ died for the ungodly. For scarcely for a righteous man will one die; yet perhaps for a good man

someone would even dare to die. But God demonstrates His own love toward us, in that while we were still sinners, Christ died for us.

Now look at this… Why would Paul say this if we are wrong? He says that Christ died, not for righteous people, not even good people, but He did it for even the lowliest, most wretched sinners. Then look what he says next… ***verses 9-10...***

Much more then, having now been justified by His blood, we shall be saved from wrath through Him. For if when we were enemies we were reconciled to God through the death of His Son, much more, having been reconciled, we shall be saved by His life.

He says that Jesus did this while we were His enemies. We were taught, by our CAM teachers, that the day you give your life to Jesus is the same day that you are forgiven and reconciled to God.

Here Paul says that we were reconciled to God at the cross and that He forgave us <u>before</u> we decided to love Him.

He loved us first.

You see, this reflects the Jesus that was described to us the day He was crucified. He was punched, kicked, whipped, stripped, stabbed, mocked, and returned nothing but compassion for them.

He died for His enemies.

He forgave them whether they asked for it or not.

They cursed Him, He blessed them.

They hated Him, He loved them.

Anyone can love someone that loves them back, but to love and forgive someone who hates you is what makes Him different from us.

Sure, we have a hard time understanding it. It makes no sense to us that He would let someone, who spent their entire life hating Him and doing evil, have eternal life, but this is His choice. He is God and can forgive whomever He wants.

This is exactly the point Paul makes in ***Romans 9:15-26***

For He says to Moses, "I WILL HAVE MERCY ON WHOMEVER I WILL HAVE MERCY, AND I WILL HAVE COMPASSION ON WHOMEVER I WILL HAVE COMPASSION." So then it is not of him who wills, nor of him who runs, but of God who shows mercy. For the Scripture says to the Pharaoh, "FOR THIS VERY PURPOSE I HAVE RAISED YOU UP, THAT I MAY SHOW MY POWER IN YOU, AND THAT MY NAME MAY BE DECLARED IN ALL THE EARTH." Therefore He has mercy on whom He wills, and whom He wills He hardens. You will say to me then, "Why does He still find fault? For who has resisted His will?" But indeed, O man, who are you to reply against God? Will the thing formed say to him who formed it, "Why have you made me like this?" Does not the potter have power over the clay, from the same lump to make one vessel for honor and another for dishonor? What if God, wanting to show His wrath and to make His power known, endured with much longsuffering the vessels of wrath prepared for destruction, and that He might make known the riches of His glory on the vessels of mercy, which He had prepared beforehand for glory, even us whom He called, not of the Jews only, but also of the Gentiles? As He says also in Hosea: "I WILL

CALL THEM MY PEOPLE, WHO WERE NOT MY PEOPLE, AND HER BELOVED, WHO WAS NOT BELOVED." "AND IT SHALL COME TO PASS IN THE PLACE WHERE IT WAS SAID TO THEM, 'YOU ARE NOT MY PEOPLE,' THERE THEY SHALL BE CALLED SONS OF THE LIVING GOD."

Here, Paul says ***"So then it is not of him who wills, nor of him who runs, but of God who shows mercy"***. This is exactly the point of this entire chapter. It is up to God, not up to you.

Moving on, verses ***12-15 of Romans 5...***

Therefore, <u>just as</u> through one man sin entered the world, and death through sin, and thus death spread to all men, because all sinned—(For until the law sin was in the world, but sin is not imputed when there is no law. Nevertheless death reigned from Adam to Moses, even over those who had not sinned according to the likeness of the transgression of Adam, who is a type of Him who was to come. But the free gift is not like the offense. For if by the one man's offense many died, much more the grace of God and the gift by the grace of the one Man, Jesus Christ, abounded to many.

Notice how he starts this passage… "just as".

"Just as" means "the same way that".

Paul says here that the gift came the same way that sin came.

Sin came because one man, Adam, chose to disobey.

When sin came, it came upon us ALL.

The free gift came the same way.

One man, Jesus, made a choice to obey God even unto death, and because of His choice and NOT yours, the gift came to ALL.

Yes, I read the verse 15 where you see the word “many”.

You should notice that the word “many” is used for both the recipients of sin and the gift.

So how “many” received sin as a result of Adam’s choice?

ALL, right?

The free gift came the same way and to the same many.

The Greek word and for this English word “many” is polus or polos and can mean part, or most, or common which is ALL. It just means a group. It is up to you to decide what the original intent was of this word. Let’s read further and we will see more evidence of Paul’s intention for this word to mean “ALL”. ***Romans 5:16-18...***

And the gift is not like that which came through the one who sinned. For the judgment which came from one offense resulted in condemnation, but the free gift which came from many offenses resulted in justification. For if by the one man's offense death reigned through the one, much more those who receive abundance of grace and of the gift of righteousness will reign in life through the One, Jesus Christ.) Therefore, as through one man's offense judgment came to all men, resulting in condemnation, even so through one Man's righteous act the free gift came to all men, resulting in justification of life.

Did Paul just say that “Judgment” came to ALL men?

But we were taught that "Judgment Day" was in the future.

How can "Judgment" come before "Judgment Day"?

We will be discussing that in next chapter, but for now, look at how he words this.

He repeats himself three more times here, as he tries to get the point pounded in our heads.

Death came by one to ALL; Life came by one to ALL. He goes on… ***Romans 5:19-21...***

For as by one man's disobedience many were made sinners, so also by one Man's obedience many will be made righteous. Moreover the law entered that the offense might abound. But where sin abounded, grace abounded much more, so that as sin reigned in death, even so grace might reign through righteousness to eternal life through Jesus Christ our Lord.

There's that word "many" again in verse 19. I hope we've cleared that up that the intention of the word is "ALL", even though King James men may have thought otherwise.

Look at verse 20... "***Moreover the law entered, that the offense might abound".***

What does Paul mean here?

It almost sounds like he is saying that God gave us the law so that we would sin more. I don't believe that is the case. I believe he is simply repeating something he said earlier in this chapter, that even though sin was here before the law came, it wasn't identified as being sin until the written Law was made manifest.

In other words, more sin can be identified because we have this book of rules to show us what sin is. The point of this verse is the end though.

Paul says that even though the Law revealed an enormous amount of sin, EVERYWHERE sin abounded (notice the past tense), Grace did much more abound.

Why does he use past tense?

It is because he is referring to "Judgment Day".

ALL were found to have sin on Judgment Day because the Law was so broad scoped that it included everyone, but everywhere sin was identified, there was an even greater amount of Grace identified by the New Covenant.

Don't believe me??

Read this… ***2Timothy 1:8-10…***

Therefore do not be ashamed of the testimony of our Lord, nor of me His prisoner, but share with me in the sufferings for the gospel according to the power of God, who has saved us and called us with a holy calling, not according to our works, but according to His own purpose and grace which was given to us in Christ Jesus before time began, but has now been revealed by the appearing of our Savior Jesus Christ, who has abolished death and brought life and immortality to light through the gospel,

This passage says so much. I just have to repeat it in my own words…

"*God saved us and called us, NOT because we deserved it, but rather because He wanted to. He gave us Grace in Christ, BEFORE TIME BEGAN, but just now revealed it by sending us Jesus who has given us the New Covenant to shed light on our condition of life and immortality."*

Sin was here before the first covenant revealed it, everyone agrees on that.

What the CAM disagrees with is that grace was always here too, but wasn't revealed until the New Covenant.

This means that it was God's intention from the beginning to forgive us ALL and let us ALL live with Him forever.

The Final Step on the Romans Road…

The last step in the Romans Road is one that is brought up a lot in discussions we have. Let's read it again… ***Romans 10:9-10, and 13...***

that if you confess with your mouth the Lord Jesus and believe in your heart that God has raised Him from the dead, you will be saved. For with the heart one believes unto righteousness, and with the mouth confession is made unto salvation.

For "WHOEVER CALLS ON THE NAME OF THE LORD SHALL BE SAVED."

We already covered this in chapter 2, but it also fits here, so let's review it again.

If you just read the text shown here and listen to the entire explanation they give you, then it makes perfect sense the way they say it. But just like everything else, you have to read the whole thought in order to understand the intentions of the writer.

These verses read alone sound like you have to take action in order to be "saved".

It seems to contradict what we are saying.

The problem with the popular theory on the meaning of this passage is in the word "saved". This word has become so popular as it is used to describe the supposed final result of the process defined by these verses in the Romans Road, but we find that the word is used a few different ways and is not always referring to the commonly accepted meaning.

Sometimes the Bible says things like "God saved us" as in the verse we just read in 2Timothy1. Obviously in that verse it means that we were saved from Death (and Hell for those who haven't read chapter 5 yet).

In Romans 10, however, it means something very different.

Let's go to the beginning of the chapter to show you what I mean… ***Romans 10:1-4...***

Brethren, my heart's desire and prayer to God for Israel is that they may be saved. For I bear them witness that they have a zeal for God, but not according to knowledge. For they being ignorant of God's righteousness, and seeking to establish their own righteousness, have not submitted to the righteousness of God. For Christ is the end of the law for righteousness to everyone who believes.

In verse one, Paul says he wishes that Israel would be saved, but from what?

He says they have a zeal for God, but not according to knowledge. This means that although they Love God and want to please Him, they don't know what has really happened.

He goes on to say that they are ignorant or unaware of the righteousness that God has now revealed to us. Instead of understanding what Jesus did and accepting it as truth, they try to establish their own righteousness by attempting to comply with the law.

The last verse here sums up Paul's intentions in this chapter.

He says that Christ is the END OF THE LAW, for ALL who believe.

What does this mean?

Paul is saying that anyone who understands that Jesus was 100% victorious also understands that the former covenant called the Law is over. If one doesn't believe that Jesus already accomplished this task, they will spend their life trying to become righteous on their own rather than just accepting Jesus' victory.

Of course CAM members will tell you that you MUST accept what Jesus did.

Acceptance and belief is definitely encouraged in the scriptures, but not as a means to be found righteous.

You are right with God because of one thing… Jesus' decision to go through with the plan.

Taken on its own, this passage, Romans 10:9-13, does seem to indicate a necessary action on your part, but read it with the rest of the chapter and you will see that Paul is merely showing us why he hopes people will believe in Jesus.

Truth Needs No Supporters

Remember, truth needs no supporters to remain the truth.

Jesus tasted death for ALL whether anyone believes it or not.

Believing that Jesus saved the world is the only thing that will end the power of the law IN YOUR HEAD.

If you think that you have a choice in the matter then you will live in fear, forever worrying about your friends and family and yourself.

God doesn't want you to bear that burden.

Jesus said His yoke is easy and His burden is light.

It is definitely no light burden thinking that you are in control of your eternal destination and possibly in control of your friends and families eternal life.

Believing that some people will die and burn in hell for all of eternity is a very torturous idea for Christians.

It is horrible and unnecessary.

Beyond the Romans Road

Moving beyond the very crooked, bumpy Romans Road, let's look at other passages that indicate that a choice was made for you. After all, Jesus did make a decision, did He not? Why did Adams decision effect ALL, but Christ's decision didn't? That idea is not at all logical.

Check this out in ***Ephesians 1:3-11...***

> ***Blessed be the God and Father of our Lord Jesus***

Christ, who has blessed us with every spiritual blessing in the heavenly places in Christ, just as <u>He chose us in Him before the foundation of the world</u>, that we should be holy and without blame before Him in love, having predestined us to adoption as sons by Jesus Christ to Himself, <u>according to the good pleasure of His will</u>, to the praise of the glory of His grace, <u>by which He made us accepted in the Beloved</u>. In Him we have redemption through His blood, the forgiveness of sins, according to the riches of His grace <u>which He made to abound toward us</u> in all wisdom and prudence, <u>having made known to us the mystery of His will</u>, <u>according to His good pleasure which He purposed in Himself</u>, that in the dispensation of the fullness of the times He might gather together in one all things in Christ, both which are in heaven and which are on earth—in Him. In Him also we have obtained an inheritance, being <u>predestined according to the purpose of Him who works all things according to the counsel of His will</u>,

Now read it again! Paul wrote a lot here. There are several points I would like to make right here before we move on to the next passage.

First of all, I underlined the parts of the sentences that clearly indicate choices that God made on our behalf.

The first one is enough to at least make someone consider that the CAM is wrong.

"***He chose us in Him before the foundation of the world***".

Wait a second; I thought we had to choose Him?

Why would Paul word things like this?

What other point could he be making?

He chose us before He made the world. He chose us to be His family before He even made Adam!!

That means that He knew before He placed the first drop of water on the earth that YOU were going to exist.

If He knew that, then He knows ALL things before they happen. What would you think of a person who makes a decision to conceive a baby, and then once it is born, takes it and tosses it into a fire? Would you consider that person to be loving and caring? No way! Well, if God creates people, knowing that they will fail (because He created us human), and then when they do, decides to burn them, that is not consistent with love and care.

Notice the part where Paul says "***He made us accepted in the Beloved***".

God made us accepted when He sent His son Jesus to the cross.

HE MADE US THAT WAY!

How does one become accepted in any scenario???

Have you always been and/or felt accepted in all situations?

Let's use logic here.

Who decides who is accepted in any situation?

Is it the acceptor, or the accepted?

It is up to me whether I accept you. You might want me to accept you, but that decision will always fall on the one who does the accepting.

I know, I know, the CAM says that God has laid out the terms of His decision to accept us.

It is true there are two covenants that He considers when deciding if you will be accepted.

Number one is the Law and guess what...? You failed miserably.

The Good News is that the Second Covenant replaced the first one. According to this one, God sees you in a new light, the light of Jesus and His choice to MAKE you right.

Look what else Paul says in this passage… "***that in the dispensation of the fullness of the times He might gather together in one all things in Christ, both which are in heaven and which are on earth"…*** We will be discussing this in the next chapter in further detail, but Paul seems to indicate his belief that the "fullness of the times" was fulfilled by Christ's work on the cross. He also says here that God's plan included gathering ALL things in Christ. You will find several passages in the Bible that say "in Jesus" or "in Christ". The CAM explains these passages to mean that those who are "in" are "in" because they chose to be "in". Here, however, Paul says God's plan was to bring ALL things "in Christ".

Look at what Paul says in the last verse of this passage… "***according to the purpose of Him who works all things according to the counsel of His will"***

Is Paul confused here?

Did he mean something other than what he said?

Does God work out ALL things according to the counsel of His own will?

If so, then God makes choices for you.

Dead in Your Sins? Good Time to be Born Again

In the beginning of this chapter, we mentioned a few passages that are often used by CAM members to argue their theory of choice. Let's look into this one found in ***John 3:3...***

> ***Jesus answered and said to him, "Most assuredly, I say to you, unless one is born again, he cannot see the kingdom of God."***

Do you remember Nicodemus' reply? ***John 3:4...***

> ***Nicodemus said to Him, "How can a man be born when he is old? Can he enter a second time into his mother's womb and be born?"***

Very good question Nicodemus!!!

How is one to become "Born Again"?

Is it their choice?

This analogy was chosen very carefully by Jesus to prove that your choice is not relevant in this particular matter concerning the Kingdom of God.

Why do we say that?

First of all, the fact that He is comparing this "change" to birth is a clue.

What choice did you have in your being born physically?

Obviously it was not by your will that you are living. It is because of the choice of your parents that you live today.

Here Jesus tells Nicodemus that we must be "Born" again!

It is right for Nicodemus to be confused considering the analogy.

Let's see if we can clarify what He meant by this term "Born Again".

Remember this from chapter 2... ***John 8:24...***

Therefore I said to you that you will die in your sins; for if you do not believe that I am He, you will die in your sins.

In chapter 2, we showed you that Jesus was referring to the time frame of when He was on the cross.

He said that whoever didn't believe WHEN He left (His death on the cross), they would die in their sins.

Then we showed you that when the time for Him to die came, ALL of His closest friends left Him, indicating that no one believed (at least not enough to take action), so ALL died in their sins.

Now, dying in your sins sounds like a very bad thing, but look what Paul says here in ***Ephesians 2:4-6...***

But God, who is rich in mercy, because of His great love with which He loved us, even when we were dead in trespasses, made us alive together with Christ (by grace you have been saved), and raised us up together, and made us sit together in the heavenly places

in Christ Jesus

Paul says here that when we were dead in our sins (while Jesus was dead), God MADE us alive WITH Jesus.

When Jesus rose from the dead, so did we.

He was dead and then made alive.

We were dead with Him, and made alive with Him.

Again, read it the way it was translated in the New Living Translation…

4 But God is so rich in mercy, and he loved us so much, 5 that even though we were dead because of our sins, he gave us life <u>when he raised Christ from the dead</u>. (It is only by God's grace that you have been saved!) 6 For he raised us from the dead along with Christ and seated us with him in the heavenly realms because we are united with Christ Jesus.

Obviously God made the choice for us.

When Jesus died, ALL died.

When Jesus was given new life (Born Again), so were we!!!

It is not your choice.

Jesus alone is the way.

It is not Jesus + Your Choice = The Way, but rather Jesus = The Way. ***John 14:6...***

Jesus said to him, "I am the way, the truth, and the life. No one comes to the Father except through Me.

Jesus is the Way, and it was by His choice.

When He died, you died.

You were given new life (born again) when God raised Christ from the dead!!!

<u>Does God hold us to a higher standard than Himself?</u>

According to the CAM, we must ask God to forgive us for our sins. At first this seems reasonable, but consider the flipside of this.

Ask any CAM leader what you are supposed to do if someone wrongs you in some way. Most of them will tell you that we are supposed to forgive everyone, no matter what they do to us.

What if they do not ask us to forgive them?

It does not matter; we are supposed to forgive them.

If that is true, then why do some believe that God doesn't forgive everyone, no matter what they do?

It is a two sided standard that doesn't make sense.

The truth is simple…

God would not ask you to do something that He is either incapable of or unwilling to do.

The Good News is that God wanted to forgive you and that is why He sent Jesus. His forgiveness is unconditional as is His love.

If you are ever confused on this issue, consider the day Jesus went to the cross.

Then ask yourself what God would do if you punched Him in the face.

The answer is that He would do the same thing He did that day when they did punch Him in the face…
He forgave them all the way to His own death!!!

It Is Not Your Choice…

It is never the choice of the guilty to be forgiven.

The one doing the forgiving has the power to decide who is forgiven and who is not.

For example, a man on death row may plead for his life, but the real power lies in the hands of the governor to make the choice to pardon him.

The CAM twists this logic by saying that although God has the power to forgive ALL, He has laid out His ground rules and therefore put the ball in your court so to speak.

We disagree.

Look at this passage found in ***Matthew 5:43-48...***

"You have heard that it was said, 'YOU SHALL LOVE YOUR NEIGHBOR and hate your enemy.' But I say to you, love your enemies, bless those who curse you, do good to those who hate you, and pray for those who spitefully use you and persecute you, that you may be sons of your Father in heaven; for He makes His sun rise on the evil and on the good, and sends rain on the just and on the unjust. For if you love those who love you, what reward have you? Do not even the tax collectors do the same? And if you greet your brethren only, what do you do more than others? Do not even the tax collectors do so? Therefore you shall be perfect, just as your Father in heaven is perfect.

Look closely at what Jesus is saying here!

He says that we are to treat others with Love, regardless of their actions.

Bless those who curse you?

Do good to those who hate you?

Love your enemies?

Ask a CAM member where one will spend eternity if he hates God.

Ask yourself that right now.

If I hated God, what would He do to me?

The CAM makes this question hard to answer. It is not hard to answer though. It is actually quite simple.

Hate God and He will return that hate with Love. Curse God and it will not faze Him because He loves you and only wants blessings for you. Punch God in the face and He will do the same thing He did when they punched Him in the face 2000 years ago… He will forgive you and only return love for your hate.

As Jesus said in this passage, even evil people can love those who love them back, but God is different. He is merciful to those who do not deserve or even want mercy. You do not have to ask Him to forgive you.

Jesus tells us that we are to forgive everyone who sins against us, but God doesn't do the same?

Nonsense!!!

Is it hard to believe that God would save even the worst of us?

At first it took me a while to come to this realization and to accept it.

It is unexpected.

We have been conditioned to feel guilty and undeserving of any good things.

The Good News is that God does things in a way that you would never expect and the greatest of these things is done in the hour we least expected.

THE HOUR
WE LEAST EXPECTED

CHAPTER 4

WHEN IS THE END?

In chapters 2 and 3, we discussed the fundamental beliefs of mainstream Christianity, regarding the subjects of belief in Jesus for your personal salvation from the penalties of sin, and the idea of free will as it applies to your choice as being the deciding factor for determining your final destination upon death.

We have found that some concepts taught in the CAM, (which is our acronym for the Currently Accepted Message of mainstream Christianity), are stacked on other concepts.

In other words, you can't just say that everybody goes to Heaven and that the Bible is your source of knowledge for that conclusion without dealing with other concepts like Hell, End time prophecy, the Rapture, the Lake of Fire, the prophecy of the 70 weeks of Daniel and more.

In these next three chapters, 4, 5, and 6, we will discuss what we believe to be the correct interpretation of these concepts and more.

Two thousand years of teaching can't be wrong… Can

it?

Very often we are accused of teaching something that goes against 2,000 years of teaching.

At first, I saw the point that our accusers were trying to make.

Why would God reveal something to us that very few had seen yet?

As we pondered this for a while and did a little research, we found out that we are definitely not the only people who have ever claimed to have found a truth in the Bible that was previously hidden.

In fact, if you belong to any number of the thousands of protestant Christian churches, you cannot say that what you believe has been taught for 2,000 years.

A simple historical research study will reveal that the beliefs that your faith subscribes to are closer to 500 years old rather than 2,000 years old. Up until 500 years or so ago, the Catholic Church was the only mainstream faith.

Why did that change?

Where did all of these other denominations come from?

Go look up the history of the protestant movement and you will find that sometimes it takes somebody willing to risk being called crazy to get us to open our eyes and consider that we might have been wrong.

In fact, the world has changed a lot over the past 2,000 years, and many changes have taken place as the result of new knowledge that surfaces along with people who dare to stand for the change that is necessary.

Solving Mysteries Takes Time

The truth is that it takes time to figure anything out. Consider the horrible events of 9/11/2001. Obviously on that day we had no idea what was happening. In fact, we are still searching for clues to the puzzle and as time passes. Hopefully we will learn more and more about how this all went down.

It just takes time and research to figure things out.

What happened when Jesus died and rose again 2,000 years ago should be getting clearer and clearer as time goes because that is how it works.

So how do you know you have it all right now?

I used to think I had ALL the answers.

I knew what my church believed and I actually believed it more than they did. If you would have asked me back then if I had the correct version of Christianity, I would have at least said that we had 90% or more of the Bible figured out.

HAHAHA!!!

Today, will I tell you I am right?

No way!!!

I will tell you that I think I'm right.

I am brave enough to debate my newfound faith against what I used to believe, but to say that you are right is to say that you know it all and have nothing left to learn.

I am not willing to make that statement again.

Only God is 100% right.

Until we are like Him, we must be willing to consider that we might be 100% wrong.

Are you like Him yet?

If not, then you might want to think about having an open mind and realize that anything is possible.

Scary stuff!!!

The soon coming end of the world is something I have heard about all of my life. In fact, it is a very popular subject throughout the entire world.

Thousands of movies, books and sermons have been produced with many interpretations as to how this final event will take place.

Does the Bible have anything to say about the end of the world?

I thought you would never ask.

If you ask a CAM member or leader about the end of the world, they will most likely tell you that it is coming very soon and that it is going to be awful for anyone who does not believe in Jesus.

But for those who have been wise enough to choose Him as their personal Savior, they say it will be the great day in which we will move to our new home where the streets are paved with gold and the gates are made of pearls.

I have believed this to be true since I was 7 years old. It wasn't until the age of 31 in 2007 that I finally had a reason to ask the question, "But where do they get this information?"

In this chapter, we will be looking at a few key passages and to see if the end is near or if we are merely dealing with more possible misinterpretations.

The New Heaven… Streets of Gold???

Let's begin our journey to the end by looking at the last book of the Bible, Revelations.

In this book, the author is describing the things he sees in a vision from God. When he gets to chapter 21, he sees some awesome, dramatic stuff happen.

He sees the passing of Heaven and Earth. He sees a New Heaven and Earth form. Then he sees a city floating down from the sky, landing on the Earth. It is the New Jerusalem.

Then he hears a voice out of Heaven say that everything is different now and there will be no more tears, no more death, and no more pain. Then one of the angels takes him in for a closer view of the city. It is made of jasper, and sapphires, and pearls and emeralds, and even the streets were paved with pure gold.

When I read this passage for the first time, I saw the same thing that my preacher had taught in church, which is a beautiful place to live forever.

But is that what this part of the vision is referring to?

Before we show you what we found, let's go back to the beginning of this book for just a second … ***Revelation 1:1...***

The Revelation of Jesus Christ, which God gave Him to show His servants—things which must shortly take place. And He sent and signified it by His angel to His servant John,

When I first began to question the CAM, I knew that the book of Revelations would have to be a very large part of our study.

At first, I was nervous about it, but I refused to just skip the parts of the Bible that seemed difficult and only look at the "easy" books.

One day, I decided to just dive into it and just see what I would find. As I did in every other part of my new study, I decided to read it as if it was my first time ever reading it.

If this was the only book I had in front of me, and I had never been taught by anyone what it meant, what would I get? Let's just see.

Rev 1:1 A Revelation of Jesus Christ,

This sentence fragment is the subject of the book. The word "revelation", in this passage, comes from the Greek word "apokalupsis", which means "disclosure". According to dictionary.com, the English word "revelation" means "to reveal or disclose something that has not been realized".

With that in mind, I saw that this book is the full "disclosure" of Jesus, or the revealing of something about Jesus that we did not know before. Going on…

which God gave Him to show His servants—things which must shortly take place. And He sent and signified it by His angel to His servant John,

This part of the sentence is often interpreted to mean that the events that are described in this "disclosure" have not happened yet.

Often the phrase "***shortly take place***" has been believed to mean that the events were to happen soon after the "disclosure" was <u>written</u>, or that when the events began, they would happen very quickly.

Either of these explanations seems possible, especially given that the CAM has spent so much time on this subject, but as with everything, we want to encourage you not to assume anything to be true or untrue until you have looked into every possible answer.

<u>When was this "Revelation" given?</u>

The first thing I would like to point out here is a very huge piece of the puzzle.

For a long time, the Book of Revelations has been considered to be the account of how things will happen in the future when Jesus is finally ready to finish things up.

The reason we have believed that for so long is because we have developed ideas about what the world will be like and look like once He has finished.

Because the things that we see with our eyes do not match the visions in our heads, meaning we do not see what we expect to see, we will always see things as unfinished.

Remember that Jesus is still not believed to be the Messiah by many because He was not what they expected Him to be. So if they were wrong about the Messiah, is it possible that what we are expecting to happen could happen in a way that we least expect?

We already believe that it will happen in an hour we least expect, so how do we know that we have the "how it will happen" figured out?

The fact that John doesn't get the vision and write these things down until way after Jesus has left the Earth has led to some confusion also.

Because the first verse says "must shortly come to pass", combined with the timing of John's writing of the vision, this leads us to believe that the events described in this vision will happen AFTER John writes the vision down.

What we now hope to clarify is that God gave this "disclosure" to Jesus first, not John and that the phrase "must shortly come to pass" is in reference to the timing of the Revelation being given to Jesus, not John.

In other words, we are questioning whether this vision "must shortly come to pass" after it was given to Jesus or it "must shortly come to pass" after it was given to John to write down.

Look at how the verse reads and you will see that it is given to John last. I've heard CAM teachers state this before but I did not see the significance of it until now.

If it was only given to John after Jesus left, then we might be wrong, but because it was given to Jesus first, then sent to John by an angel brings a new question to mind.

When was this "disclosure" given to Jesus?

When it was given to John, you will see very soon, is irrelevant. Let's read this part again…

which God gave Him to show His servants—things which must shortly take place.

My version…

"Which God gave to Jesus to show His servants things that were about to happen"

When you think about the verse this way the phrase "things that must shortly come to pass", moves to a different position in time.

This leads us to ask the question:

When did God give this "disclosure" to Jesus?

Have you ever even thought to ask that question?

I never even thought to ask that question until now.

So when did it happen?

Let's flip our Bibles back to ***Matthew 24:3…***

Now as He sat on the Mount of Olives, the disciples came to Him privately, saying, "Tell us, when will these things be? And what will be the sign of Your coming, and of the end of the age?"

Here, the disciples, (Jesus servants), ask Jesus when the end of the age will be and what will it look like.

Jesus goes on to answer these questions by describing several events that we find also described in the book of Revelations.

For example… Matthew 24:29-30

"Immediately after the tribulation of those days the sun will be darkened, and the moon will not give its light; the stars will fall from heaven, and the powers of the heavens will be shaken. Then the sign of the Son of Man will appear in heaven, and then all the tribes of the earth will mourn, and they will see the Son of Man coming on the clouds of heaven with power and great glory.

Compare this passage in Matthew to ***Revelations 6:12-13...***

I looked when He opened the sixth seal, and behold, there was a great earthquake; and the sun became black as sackcloth of hair, and the moon became like blood. And the stars of heaven fell to the earth, as a fig tree drops its late figs when it is shaken by a mighty wind.

So again, I have to ask you… When was Jesus given this "disclosure"?

The whole idea, that God had to give Jesus anything, tells us that at one point in time, Jesus did not have all the answers. It is really never talked about, but when did Jesus learn all of these things regarding what He was supposed to do and when? Was He just born with this knowledge? When He was 3 years old was He thinking about how He was going to die on a cross? Or was this knowledge given to Him a little at a time as He grew up?

Obviously He knew what was up before He answered the questions of the disciples in Matthew 24.

Obviously by this point in His life, He knew ALL things as God knows ALL things.

My guess is that Jesus was clued into these things around the beginning of His ministry that started when He was baptized by John the Baptist and then spent the next 40 days in the wilderness. It seems like a good time to me to let Him in on the full plan, but regardless of the exact time of this "disclosure" being given to Jesus, it must have been given prior to this time when He described it to the disciples. So let's read it again with the thought that God gave this "revelation" to Jesus before Jesus speaks in Matthew 24...

Let's look at Rev 1:1 again, but this time, I'm going to add, in parenthesis, some clarifying words…

The Revelation of Jesus Christ, which God gave Him (at the beginning of His ministry) ***to show His servants—***(the disciples) ***things which must shortly take place.***

Jesus was given this "Revelation" so that He could tell His disciples what was about to happen.

How else could Jesus have quoted things that are in Revelations without having read it?

The fact that John doesn't get this vision until well after Jesus is gone only lends to the timelessness of God.

Why is this important?

You will see why very soon, but first we need to make a few more points, so please stick with us here…

John's Flashback

If you read the first chapter of Revelations closely, you will see that John was on the island of Patmos and "was in the Spirit on the Lord's Day". Look up the definition of the words "Lord's Day" here and you will see that this was not a Sabbath day or a Sunday, but rather the day that belonged to the Lord.

What day it was when John had this vision is irrelevant, because "in the spirit" he was taken to the "Lord's Day" and then shown the disclosure.

We believe that John had a flashback vision that was given to him to "disclose" the events that took place at the cross and resurrection which was the "Lord's Day".

We hope that our explanation of how this disclosure was given to Jesus first will cause you to realize that when this was given to John is not so important, but when it was given to Jesus is what really matters.

We know it had to be before He died, but at the beginning of His ministry seems like a good time to tell Him, so let's use that to show what we are getting at (if you haven't already figured that out).

Is the book of Revelations literal or symbolic?

Ask just about any CAM member or teacher and they will tell you that Revelations is very symbolic but also contains passages that are meant to be taken literally.

I used to see that as being true, but as with anything, the power of suggestion will often cause you to overlook things that are in plain sight.

If the leader you trust says that this is literal, you will most likely never even think to second guess his/her opinion.

We hope that you will see some things in this section that will at minimum cause you to consider the possibilities that you were misled. As we said earlier, it is always best to consider every possibility and do not make a decision until you have heard all sides of the story first.

Let's look at the last part of this passage… ***Revelations 1:1...***

> ***And He sent and signified it by His angel to His***

servant John,

Not only is the timing of this disclosure a big clue, but the word "signified" in this verse is also big deal.

I have never heard any CAM teacher point this word out when discussing this book.

You will not find this word in every English translation, but it is present in the Greek as the word "sēmainō".

I don't know why some versions leave it out, unless the translators just failed to see the word as significant.

The word "signify" means "to make known by signs".

As soon as you begin to get into this book it becomes very clear that this vision is written in signs and symbols when the writer begins transcribing what he sees.

Here are a few obvious examples:

Revelations 1:12-16...

Then I turned to see the voice that spoke with me. And having turned I saw seven golden lampstands, and in the midst of the seven lampstands One like the Son of Man, clothed with a garment down to the feet and girded about the chest with a golden band. His head and hair were white like wool, as white as snow, and His eyes like a flame of fire; His feet were like fine brass, as if refined in a furnace, and His voice as the sound of many waters; He had in His right hand seven stars, out of His mouth went a sharp two-edged sword, and His countenance was like the sun shining in its strength.

This is the first thing that John sees.

Is it symbolic or literal?

The symbolism is explained a couple verses later…
Revelations 1:19-20...

Write the things which you have seen, and the things which are, and the things which will take place after this. The mystery of the seven stars which you saw in My right hand, and the seven golden lampstands: The seven stars are the angels of the seven churches, and the seven lampstands which you saw are the seven churches.

Here the one speaking, Jesus, tells John to write down the things he has seen already, and whatever he sees now and finally whatever else he sees after this.

You see, John "saw" lamp stands.

He didn't see seven churches.

Clearly this is symbolism.

What about this? ***Revelations 12:1-4...***

Now a great sign appeared in heaven: a woman clothed with the sun, with the moon under her feet, and on her head a garland of twelve stars. Then being with child, she cried out in labor and in pain to give birth. And another sign appeared in heaven: behold, a great, fiery red dragon having seven heads and ten horns, and seven diadems on his heads. His tail drew a third of the stars of heaven and threw them to the earth. And the dragon stood before the woman who was ready to give birth, to devour her Child as soon as it was born.

He said “a great sign appeared in heaven”.

Was this woman literal or symbolic?

What about the dragon?

He sweeps a third of the stars from the sky!

That is a big dragon.

Read this whole “disclosure” and you will find obvious symbolism on every page. With so much symbolism, how do we know which parts are to be taken literally?

John sees a dragon, two separate beasts, and several horses galloping across the sky.

Towards the end of the book, he sees a city made of gold floating down to the New Earth.

Is that literal?

I was taught that it was. I would venture that 99% of CAM teachers will claim that it is literal.

What do they base this claim on?

Does the writer of this book tell us to take it literally?

If the writer did not mention anything regarding how this is to be taken, then we might be able to assume that it is possible that it is literal.

The problem I have with this is that the writer DID say something about it, and in the very first verse.

This message has been "signified" or formatted in a symbolic code that cannot be taken at face value, but is to be interpreted.

The New Jerusalem… a Literal City, or Something Else?

Let's jump back again towards the end of this book and read about the city we started writing about in the beginning of this chapter… ***Revelations 21:1-4...***

Now I saw a new heaven and a new earth, for the first heaven and the first earth had passed away. Also there was no more sea. Then I, John, saw the holy city, New Jerusalem, coming down out of heaven from God, prepared as a bride adorned for her husband. And I heard a loud voice from heaven saying, "Behold, the tabernacle of God is with men, and He will dwell with them, and they shall be His people. God Himself will be with them and be their God. And God will wipe away every tear from their eyes; there shall be no more death, nor sorrow, nor crying. There shall be no more pain, for the former things have passed away."

Here John sees a new heaven and earth.

Could this be symbolic?

Then he sees the holy city coming down from Heaven.

What is this city?

Is it where we will live in the future like the CAM teaches?

Look at what John says in ***verse 9...***

Then one of the seven angels who had the seven bowls filled with the seven last plagues came to me and

talked with me, saying, "Come, I will show you the bride, the Lamb's wife."

Look at the words I underlined here, "***the Lamb's wife***".

Who is the Lamb's wife?

John sees the city "***prepared as a bride adorned for her husband***" and then the angel calls the city "***the Lamb's wife***".

So what is going on here?

Is this a literal city, or is it symbolic?

Remember that the first verse in this book says that this message is symbolic.

Could it be that this is symbolic?

Most CAM leaders will tell you that we will live in this city forever.

Most Christians, when asked to describe what heaven looks like, will describe in detail this city.

They believe this city is literal, but the angel calls it "***the Lamb's wife***".

We were taught that the bride of Christ is a symbolic term for God's people.

Obviously there is some symbolism here, but what does it mean?

Is this a city, or God's people?

Is Jesus going to marry some golden streets?

Let's refer to some other Bible passages and see if we can make sense of this.

O Jerusalem

In the Old Testament, when God was speaking to His people, He said things like this in ***Isaiah 52:1...***

Awake! Awake! Put on your strength, Zion; put on your beautiful robes, O Jerusalem, the holy city. For never again shall come to you uncircumcised and unclean ones.

In this verse, God is speaking to "Jerusalem".

Is He talking to the city, meaning the buildings and streets, or is He using the name of the city symbolically in reference to the people of the city?

Obviously He is talking to the people.

Jerusalem is a real city, but city names are very commonly used symbolically. For example, if you have ever been to a concert, often the band leader will at some point yell out "Hello New York City!!!" and all of the people who identify with the city will shout back.

That is what is happening in this verse.

God is using the name of the city symbolically.

So now back to Revelations, the angel shows John the New Jerusalem.

Is it a literal city?

If so, why does the angel call it the bride which is obviously a term to reference His people?

The New Jerusalem is symbolic of God's people who were made New.

Rev 21:10...

And he carried me away in the Spirit to a great and high mountain, and showed me the great city, the holy Jerusalem, descending out of heaven from God,

The New Deal!!!

The city is symbolic of God's people.

Jerusalem was symbolic of God's people in the Old Testament, now God's people are symbolized by the New Jerusalem.

Why is it new?

The city is new because the Old Covenant is gone and, because of Jesus, everything was made New.

The new heaven, the new earth, and the new city are all symbolic of something new.

Look at how the writer explains this newness in ***verse 4...***

... for the first things passed away.

The NIV says "***for the old order of things has passed away***"

The new heaven and earth and city are symbols of something

made new, "***for the old order of things has passed away***".

What "old order" has passed away?

What is something that was old that was used for "order" that has now been made new?

Look at what the writer of Hebrews says about something that was Old that has been replaced by something new. ***Hebrews 8:6-13...***

But now He has obtained a more excellent ministry, inasmuch as He is also Mediator of a better covenant, which was established on better promises. For if that first covenant had been faultless, then no place would have been sought for a second. Because finding fault with them, He says: "BEHOLD, THE DAYS ARE COMING, SAYS THE LORD, WHEN I WILL MAKE A NEW COVENANT WITH THE HOUSE OF ISRAEL AND WITH THE HOUSE OF JUDAH— NOT ACCORDING TO THE COVENANT THAT I MADE WITH THEIR FATHERS IN THE DAY WHEN I TOOK THEM BY THE HAND TO LEAD THEM OUT OF THE LAND OF EGYPT; BECAUSE THEY DID NOT CONTINUE IN MY COVENANT, AND I DISREGARDED THEM, SAYS THE LORD. FOR THIS IS THE COVENANT THAT I WILL MAKE WITH THE HOUSE OF ISRAEL AFTER THOSE DAYS, SAYS THE LORD: I WILL PUT MY LAWS IN THEIR MIND AND WRITE THEM ON THEIR HEARTS; AND I WILL BE THEIR GOD, AND THEY SHALL BE MY PEOPLE. NONE OF THEM SHALL TEACH HIS NEIGHBOR, AND NONE HIS BROTHER, SAYING, 'KNOW THE LORD,' FOR ALL SHALL KNOW ME, FROM THE LEAST OF THEM TO THE GREATEST OF THEM. FOR I WILL BE MERCIFUL TO THEIR

UNRIGHTEOUSNESS, AND THEIR SINS AND THEIR LAWLESS DEEDS I WILL REMEMBER NO MORE." In that He says, "A NEW COVENANT," He has made the first obsolete. Now what is becoming obsolete and growing old is ready to vanish away.

The writer of Hebrews says here that the Old Covenant, which is the Law, has been replaced by a new one.

That sounds like "***the old order of things has passed away"*** to me.

In other words, it is a whole new world since Jesus died and rose again and gave us the New Covenant.

The old way was made obsolete and now we live in the new world.

Even our calendar started over that day.

The New Heaven and Earth and City are symbolic of the New Covenant which replaced the Old one.

When Jesus died, the Old Covenant died with Him, but when He rose again, everything was made new with the confirmation of the New Covenant.

Remember this verse we read in chapter 2, ***2Corinthians 5:17...***

Therefore, if anyone is in Christ, he is a new creation; old things have passed away; behold, all things have become new.

The Old things have passed away and ALL things have become new. This is just another example of what happened when the Old Covenant was replaced with the New Covenant.

Not One Little Thing…

Are you still not convinced that the New Jerusalem and heaven and earth are symbolic of the end of the Law or Old Covenant?

Then let's jump to the side for just a bit so I can make another point.

Let's talk about the "Old" way.

The Law is the Old Covenant. Has any part of the Law changed since the coming of the Lord?

Many CAM teachers will agree that when the New Covenant was given to us, at the cross and resurrection of Jesus, the Law was made obsolete.

Some CAM members still cling to the Law, saying that it is still fully in effect, while others just dismiss certain parts of it.

All I'm asking now is this:

Did **ANYTHING** change regarding the Law when Jesus died and rose again?

The writer of Hebrews claimed the Old Covenant was now obsolete. That sure sounds like a change to me.

Also Peter had a vision regarding the law. Remember the vision he saw of the unclean food that God said was now clean? ***Acts 10:9-16…***

> ***The next day, as they went on their journey and***

drew near the city, Peter went up on the housetop to pray, about the sixth hour. Then he became very hungry and wanted to eat; but while they made ready, he fell into a trance and saw heaven opened and an object like a great sheet bound at the four corners, descending to him and let down to the earth. In it were all kinds of four-footed animals of the earth, wild beasts, creeping things, and birds of the air. And a voice came to him, "Rise, Peter; kill and eat." But Peter said, "Not so, Lord! For I have never eaten anything common or unclean." And a voice spoke to him again the second time, "What God has cleansed you must not call common." This was done three times. And the object was taken up into heaven again.

According to the Law, the food on this sheet was not to be eaten. In this vision, Jesus tells Peter to eat it. Peter knew it was wrong, so he resisted at first, but He insisted that He had made these foods clean.

Now some CAM members will explain that this vision was symbolic of how the Gentiles were now able to be clean if they believed in Jesus, but even that would mark a change in the Law since the Gentiles were excluded from the Old Covenant and are now included in the New.

So, if this vision was truly from God, and we can now freely eat pork, (mmm… bacon), then we must agree that something regarding the law has changed.

That being so, let's look at this verse in Matthew where there is another hidden clue that will add some weight to our claim. ***Matthew 5:18...***

For assuredly, I say to you, till heaven and earth pass away, one jot or one tittle will by no means pass from the law till all is fulfilled.

Let's clarify some things. The word "jot" here comes from the Greek word "iota" which is the name of the eighth letter of the Greek alphabet. It is used here to figuratively describe something very small. Have you ever heard someone use the term "not one iota" to mean "not one little thing"? A "tittle" is very similar. Let's reword this verse to clarify what it means…

My version…

For truly I say to you, Till the heaven and the earth pass away, not one little thing shall in any way pass from the Law until all is fulfilled.

Let me restate that again…

Until heaven and earth pass away, NOTHING about the Law will pass until ALL is fulfilled

Let me restate that again…

ALL things will be fulfilled when the Law has passed and Heaven and Earth have passed.

Again…

Heaven and Earth and the Law will pass at the same time, signifying that ALL has been fulfilled.

One more time…

When everything is finished, Heaven and Earth and the Law will pass away.

Can you see what is happening here?

Jesus says that NOTHING about the Law is going to change until Heaven and Earth pass away.

The Law changed when Jesus died!

What does that mean for Heaven and Earth?

Obviously when Jesus died, symbolically, everything died because He represented ALL of creation.

Heaven and Earth passed away when Jesus died on the Cross.

When Jesus rose again, ALL of Mankind was made New. Heaven and Earth were made New.

Everything is New today because the Old order of things, or the Law, is gone!!!

A Whole New World

Look what Paul says about Jesus here in ***Colossians 1:15-20...***

He is the image of the invisible God, the firstborn over all creation. For by Him all things were created that are in heaven and that are on earth, visible and invisible, whether thrones or dominions or principalities or powers. All things were created through Him and for Him. And He is before all things, and in Him all things consist. And He is the head of the body, the church, who is the beginning, the firstborn from the dead, that in all things He may have the preeminence. For it pleased the Father that in Him all the fullness should dwell, and by Him to reconcile all things to Himself, by Him, whether things on earth or things in heaven, having made peace through the blood of His cross.

Jesus is the creator of ALL things. By Him, through Him, and for Him, ALL things were created. Verse 19 says "***For it pleased the Father that in Him all the fullness should dwell***".

If ALL things dwell in Him, then what would happen to ALL things when He died?

ALL things would die, right?

Look what Paul says here in ***2Corinthians 5:14...***

For the love of Christ compels us, because we judge thus: that if One died for all, then all died;

We discussed this passage more in depth earlier in chapter 2. Jesus represented ALL things. **When He died, ALL things died. When He was made New, the day He rose again, ALL things were made New.**

Q. In Matthew 5:18 Jesus says that **NOTHING** shall pass from the law until when?

A. Until heaven and earth pass away.

Q. When did the Law change?

A. When Jesus gave us the New Covenant at the cross and resurrection.

Q. When did it become ok to eat pork?

A. At the cross and resurrection of Jesus.

Q. When did the old order of things pass away?

A. When Jesus passed away at the cross.

Q. When did everything become new?

A. When Jesus became new at the resurrection.

Q. When did heaven and earth pass away?

A. When Jesus passed away at the cross.

Q. When was Heaven and Earth made new?

A. When Jesus rose from the dead.

Am I making my point clear?

The New Heaven and Earth are symbolic of the New Covenant that was given to us at the cross and resurrection of Jesus. The New Jerusalem symbolizes the change that happened to us when this was accomplished.

And, look what else Jesus said in ***Matt 5:18 "until all is fulfilled".***

ALL things were fulfilled at the cross and resurrection of Jesus.

There is nothing left to be completed.

It is finished!!!

You Must Be Born Again!!!

You see, this "disclosure", known as the book of Revelations, was given to Jesus so He could tell His servants about the events that were getting ready to happen.

He was telling them these things all throughout His ministry.

All of His stories were concerning these events.

The climax of the book of Revelations is the passing of the old heaven and earth and the beginning of the new heaven and earth, just as the climax of the entire Bible is the Cross and Resurrection of Jesus.

These events in Revelations are **not** to be taken literally.

They are symbolic of the spiritual change that took place when Jesus died and rose again.

When He died, ALL of creation symbolically died, and when He was given new life, ALL of creation was "Born Again"!!

That is what Jesus was referring to when He told Nicodemus in John 3 that unless you are "Born Again", you cannot enter the kingdom of God.

The reason He used the analogy "Born Again" is because it requires nothing of you.

Think about it… What role did you play in being born? Did you make any decisions that led to your birth?

Of course you didn't. The one being born has no choice in the matter.

That is why Jesus did not explain to Nicodemus how to be born again, and neither is this process explained anywhere in the Bible, because it is not about you or your choice, but about Him and His choice that had an effect on you.

So if the new heaven and earth and the New Jerusalem symbolize the end of the Law and Beginning of the new order of things, then ALL of that has already happened!

So the "End" of the world, as referenced in the Bible, has already taken place.

There is no future "End" found other than the personal end we will each face when we die.

We will be looking into what the Bible says about what happens to us when we die in chapters 5 and 6, but for now, we want to continue to talk about the Law to further demonstrate the fact that it is now obsolete like the writer of Hebrews claimed it to be.

Moses' Ministry of Death!!!

Many CAM members will tell you that Law is obsolete. Some will say it is still in effect. Very few will claim that it is to be completely disregarded like we believe it is to be.

Even the CAM members that claim the law is obsolete, usually still cling to the Ten Commandments.

As a matter of fact, in an effort to get the public schools to display the Ten Commandments a few years ago, a certain religious TV station was featuring a special about the Ten Commandments. The show was being hosted by the owners of the network and to my disbelief, one of them made the statement that the Ten Commandments were "the single greatest gift that God ever gave to mankind".

"Seriously!!??" I wanted to ask this person.

What about Jesus?

As you will see in the next few scripture references we will be discussing, the Ten Commandments were the base of the Old Covenant.

Jesus is the base for the New Covenant.

Jesus, before He died, was representing the Old Covenant, but spoke often about the end of it.

Look what John says in the opening verses of his gospel… ***John 1:1-5, 14...***

In the beginning was the Word, and the Word was with God, and the Word was God. He was in the beginning with God. All things were made through Him, and without Him nothing was made that was made. In Him was life, and the life was the light of men. And the light shines in the darkness, and the darkness did not comprehend it…

And the <u>Word became flesh</u> and dwelt among us, and we beheld His glory, the glory as of the only begotten of the Father, full of grace and truth.

Jesus was the "Word made flesh".

What "Word" is John referring to?

Up until this point, the only written word claimed to be the word of God was the Old Testament which is the Old Covenant.

Everything in the Old Covenant is actually referring to Jesus. Here, the Old Covenant was made into a man. Look what Jesus says here in ***John 5:37-47...***

And the Father Himself, who sent Me, has testified of Me. You have neither heard His voice at any time, nor seen His form. But you do not have His word abiding in you, because whom He sent, Him you do not

believe. You search the Scriptures, for in them you think you have eternal life; and these are they which testify of Me. But you are not willing to come to Me that you may have life. "I do not receive honor from men. But I know you, that you do not have the love of God in you. I have come in My Father's name, and you do not receive Me; if another comes in his own name, him you will receive. How can you believe, who receive honor from one another, and do not seek the honor that comes from the only God? Do not think that I shall accuse you to the Father; there is one who accuses you—Moses, in whom you trust. For if you believed Moses, you would believe Me; for he wrote about Me. But if you do not believe his writings, how will you believe My words?"

Jesus says in verse 39 that the "scriptures" or the writings of the Old Testament were referring to Him. He then goes on to tell them that they never really believed in Moses (the one who obtained the Law from God) or they would believe in Him, because Moses wrote about Him.

Jesus was the Law, or the Old Covenant. When He died, so did it. The Old Covenant was never meant to be in effect forever. It was always God's plan to replace it with Jesus.

Look at what Paul says about the Old Covenant here in ***2 Corinthians 3:1-18...***

Do we begin again to commend ourselves? Or do we need, as some others, epistles of commendation to you or letters of commendation from you? You are our epistle written in our hearts, known and read by all men; clearly you are an epistle of Christ, ministered by us, written not with ink but by the Spirit of the living God, not on tablets of stone but on tablets of flesh, that is, of the heart. And we have such trust through Christ toward God. Not that we are sufficient of ourselves to think of

anything as being from ourselves, but our sufficiency is from God, <u>who also made us sufficient as ministers of the new covenant</u>, <u>not of the letter but of the Spirit</u>; <u>for the letter kills, but the Spirit gives life</u>. But if the <u>ministry of death</u>, <u>written and engraved on stones</u>, was glorious, so that the children of Israel could not look steadily at the face of Moses because of the glory of his countenance, which glory was passing away, how will the ministry of the Spirit not be more glorious? For if the ministry of condemnation had glory, the ministry of righteousness exceeds much more in glory. For even what was made glorious had no glory in this respect, because of the glory that excels. For if what is passing away was glorious, what remains is much more glorious. Therefore, since we have such hope, we use great boldness of speech—unlike Moses, who put a veil over his face so that the children of Israel could not look steadily at the end of what was passing away. But their minds were blinded. For until this day the same veil remains unlifted in the reading of the Old Testament, because the veil is taken away in Christ. But even to this day, when Moses is read, a veil lies on their heart. Nevertheless when one turns to the Lord, the veil is taken away. Now the Lord is the Spirit; and where the Spirit of the Lord is, there is liberty. But we all, with unveiled face, beholding as in a mirror the glory of the Lord, are being transformed into the same image from glory to glory, just as by the Spirit of the Lord.

In verse 6, Paul says that he has been made to be a minister of the New Covenant. He says it is "<u>not of the letter but of the Spirit</u>; <u>for the letter kills, but the Spirit gives life</u>".

The letter kills?

We were taught that this written book was life for us, but Paul says that it kills.

What did he mean by that?

In verse 7, Paul goes on to call the Ten Commandments and the Old Covenant the Ministry of Death, engraved on stones. He says that any time the Old Testament is referenced, that a "veil" lies on our hearts.

He then contrasts that in verse 17, saying that Jesus is the New Covenant of the Spirit, and He has given us Liberty. The written Law was given to us for no other reason than to bring condemnation to us all, placing us all equally in trouble.

Look what Paul says here in ***Romans 3:19,20...***

> ***Now we know that whatever the law says, it says to those who are under the law, that every mouth may be stopped, and all the world may become guilty before God. Therefore by the deeds of the law no flesh will be justified in His sight, for by the law is the knowledge of sin.***

The Law was given "that every mouth may be stopped". This means that we do not have the right to point fingers at anyone else concerning their shortcomings in reference to the Law because, as verse 20 says, no one is justified by the Law.

The Law was merely given to bring definition to sin, thereby including ALL of us as recipients of its penalties.

The Good News is that when Jesus died, the Law died too because He represented the Law and ALL of us who were subject to it.

When He rose again, the New Covenant took over, eliminating the Old Covenant.

A Better Covenant

As previously mentioned, the Old Covenant was never meant to rule forever. Look what God says about the Old Covenant here in ***Jeremiah 31:31-34...***

"Behold, the days are coming, says the LORD, when I will make a new covenant with the house of Israel and with the house of Judah— not according to the covenant that I made with their fathers in the day that I took them by the hand to lead them out of the land of Egypt, My covenant which they broke, though I was a husband to them, says the LORD. But this is the covenant that I will make with the house of Israel after those days, says the LORD: I will put My law in their minds, and write it on their hearts; and I will be their God, and they shall be My people. No more shall every man teach his neighbor, and every man his brother, saying, 'Know the LORD,' for they all shall know Me, from the least of them to the greatest of them, says the LORD. For I will forgive their iniquity, and their sin I will remember no more."

Here God says that He is going to one day give us a New Covenant. He says that it will NOT be like the one He made when He delivered His people from Egypt. The covenant He is talking about is the Law He gave Moses right after they escaped Egypt.

According to this passage, the New Covenant would be written on our hearts and minds.

This sounds very much like the way Paul describes the Old and New Covenants in 2Corinthians 3 that we just read.

Look at verse 34. It says that when the New Covenant comes, it will no longer be necessary to teach your neighbor or brother to "Know the Lord".

When the New Covenant He is describing comes, ALL will know Him, because ALL will be included in the forgiveness of their sins.

Time to Grow Up

We are often ridiculed for saying that the Law has been made obsolete.

Why is this such a bad thing?

Do we need God breathing down our necks in order for us to do what is right?

I mean, do you think that believing the Law is gone will cause some to murder?

People murder every day and I would bet that many of them are fully aware that the Ten Commandments say that it is wrong.

Here's an example of what I am trying to say…

I had this discussion with a long time preacher friend of mine.

He said to me "So you're telling me that God would not be angry if I had books of pornography on my book shelves rather than these religious books?"

I replied to him "If you knew that God would not be angry, what types of books *would* you keep on your shelves?"

The truth is simple…

By tossing the rule book out of the window, God has put the ball back into your court.

Will you do what is right simply because it is the right thing to do, or do you need God to scare you into behaving?

It is time to grow up!!!

When I first read this passage to the pastor of the church I was attending when I first began this journey, he told me that this particular covenant had not been fulfilled yet. He said this because of the wording found in this verse…
Revelations 21:3...

And I heard a loud voice from heaven saying, "Behold, the tabernacle of God is with men, and He will dwell with them, and they shall be His people. God Himself will be with them and be their God.

He was right.

This passage in Revelations does match the wording found in Jeremiah 31:33 that we just read.

The problem he was having is that he believed Revelations to be a future event, and because of its obvious parallelism with Jeremiah 31:33, this could not have already happened.

He then cornered me and asked if I really believed that this had been accomplished.

I told him that at that point in my study, I couldn't be certain, but that the writer of Hebrews seemed to think that it had been.

Check this out here in ***Hebrews 8:1-13...***

Now this is the main point of the things we are saying: We have such a High Priest, who is seated at the right hand of the throne of the Majesty in the heavens, a Minister of the sanctuary and of the true tabernacle which the Lord erected, and not man. For every high priest is appointed to offer both gifts and sacrifices. Therefore it is necessary that this One also have something to offer. For if He were on earth, He would

not be a priest, since there are priests who offer the gifts according to the law; who serve the copy and shadow of the heavenly things, as Moses was divinely instructed when he was about to make the tabernacle. For He said, "SEE THAT YOU MAKE ALL THINGS ACCORDING TO THE PATTERN SHOWN YOU ON THE MOUNTAIN." But now He has obtained a more excellent ministry, inasmuch as He is also Mediator of a better covenant, which was established on better promises. For if that first covenant had been faultless, then no place would have been sought for a second. Because finding fault with them, He says: "BEHOLD, THE DAYS ARE COMING, SAYS THE LORD, WHEN I WILL MAKE A NEW COVENANT WITH THE HOUSE OF ISRAEL AND WITH THE HOUSE OF JUDAH—NOT ACCORDING TO THE COVENANT THAT I MADE WITH THEIR FATHERS IN THE DAY WHEN I TOOK THEM BY THE HAND TO LEAD THEM OUT OF THE LAND OF EGYPT; BECAUSE THEY DID NOT CONTINUE IN MY COVENANT, AND I DISREGARDED THEM, SAYS THE LORD. FOR THIS IS THE COVENANT THAT I WILL MAKE WITH THE HOUSE OF ISRAEL AFTER THOSE DAYS, SAYS THE LORD: I WILL PUT MY LAWS IN THEIR MIND AND WRITE THEM ON THEIR HEARTS; AND I WILL BE THEIR GOD, AND THEY SHALL BE MY PEOPLE. NONE OF THEM SHALL TEACH HIS NEIGHBOR, AND NONE HIS BROTHER, SAYING, 'KNOW THE LORD,' FOR ALL SHALL KNOW ME, FROM THE LEAST OF THEM TO THE GREATEST OF THEM. FOR I WILL BE MERCIFUL TO THEIR UNRIGHTEOUSNESS, AND THEIR SINS AND THEIR LAWLESS DEEDS I WILL REMEMBER NO MORE." In that He says, "A NEW COVENANT," He has made the first obsolete. Now what is becoming

obsolete and growing old is ready to vanish away.

The writer describes the Old Covenant as faulty and then quotes Jeremiah 31:31-34, saying that this IS the New Covenant that was made for us when Jesus died and rose again.

He then says that the Old Covenant is obsolete and ready to vanish away.

So, YES, Jeremiah 31:31-34 has been fulfilled by the death and resurrection of Jesus some 2,000 years ago, which, just as my former pastor said, sounds a lot like the wording found in Revelation 21:3, which means that has been fulfilled also.

"No more shall every man teach his neighbor, and every man his brother, saying, 'Know the LORD,' for they all shall know Me, from the least of them to the greatest of them, says the LORD. For I will forgive their iniquity, and their sin I will remember no more."

As a close friend of mine pointed out the other day, there are no stipulations found in this passage. It doesn't say "If you believe" or "If you try hard" or anything. It simply states that when the New Covenant comes, it will be for everyone and include everyone.

It Is Finished!!!

Jesus was the fleshly manifestation of the writings and prophecies described in the Old Testament. He came to Earth and taught the Law and its consequences. He also talked a lot about the end of the age and what that was going to be like.

There is no way He could have talked about the end if it had never been revealed to Him. It, however, was revealed to

Him, as were ALL things. That is how He was able to describe the things written in the book of Revelations that was not penned until years after His death, resurrection, and ascension to Heaven.

Because Jesus was the Old Covenant made into Man, when that Man died, so did the Old Covenant.

The End of the World described in the Bible is symbolic of the end of the Old Order of things.

Let's look at some other passages that appear to describe the end as having already been accomplished. ***Hebrews 9:24-28...***

For Christ has not entered the holy places made with hands, which are copies of the true, but into heaven itself, now to appear in the presence of God for us; not that He should offer Himself often, as the high priest enters the Most Holy Place every year with blood of another—He then would have had to suffer often since the foundation of the world; but now, once at the end of the ages, He has appeared to put away sin by the sacrifice of Himself. And as it is appointed for men to die once, but after this the judgment, so Christ was offered once to bear the sins of many. To those who eagerly wait for Him He will appear a second time, apart from sin, for salvation.

Look at verse 26. The writer states that Jesus has appeared NOW, at the End of the Ages to "put away" sin by the sacrifice of Himself.

Doesn't this sound like the end was at the sacrificing of Jesus?

Many CAM members read verse 27, "***And as it is appointed***

for men to die once, but after this the judgment, so Christ was offered once to bear the sins of many", and say that it points to a future judgment, but what the writer is saying here is that the sentence or consequences of the judgment will be rendered to each man upon his death.

The Good News is that Jesus took all the penalties of our sin upon Himself and gave us eternal life.

The last verse here is just to give hope to those who believe in Jesus that He will be there to collect us when we die. It doesn't mean that He will not be collecting everybody when they die, but the writer is simply confirming to those who care, the ones eagerly expecting this, that they will not be disappointed.

Look what Paul writes here in ***1Timothy 1:8-10...***

Therefore do not be ashamed of the testimony of our Lord, nor of me His prisoner, but share with me in the sufferings for the gospel according to the power of God, who has saved us and called us with a holy calling, not according to our works, but according to His own purpose and grace which was given to us in Christ Jesus before time began, but has now been revealed by the appearing of our Savior Jesus Christ, who has abolished death and brought life and immortality to light through the gospel,

He says here that this Covenant was always meant for us to have, even before time began. He says that it was only revealed by the appearing of Jesus who has abolished death and brought life and immortality to light.

Remember that Paul called the Old Covenant the ministry of Death.

Now, compare this passage to Paul's letter to the Romans in ***Romans 5:12-14...***

Therefore, just as through one man sin entered the world, and death through sin, and thus death spread to all men, because all sinned—(For until the law sin was in the world, but sin is not imputed when there is no law. Nevertheless death reigned from Adam to Moses, even over those who had not sinned according to the likeness of the transgression of Adam, who is a type of Him who was to come.

Here Paul is talking about the fact that even though the Law had not been given yet, sin was still here. Sin, however was not revealed until the Old Covenant was given, which defined sin. Once the Old Covenant was given, it was obvious that sin was here, because the parameters were laid out, exposing our faults.

Now back to 1Timothy 1:8-10, Paul is saying that even though the parameters of the New Covenant were not revealed yet, doesn't mean that God's grace was not already here.

"grace which was given to us in Christ Jesus before time began, but has now been revealed by the appearing of our Savior Jesus Christ"

The grace was always here, as was sin.

The Old Covenant revealed sin to the World, just as the New Covenant has now revealed God's grace to the same World.

It is really quite simple as Paul explains in ***Romans 5:18...***

Therefore, as through one man's offense judgment came to all men, resulting in condemnation,

even so through one Man's righteous act the free gift came to all men, resulting in justification of life.

Adam sinned and brought condemnation to the entire World, and Christ reversed the effects with His act of obedience.

The End!!!

And that was the End!!!

The end of the way things used to be, the end of the "old order of things" as described in Revelations 21:4, coincides with the crucifixion of Jesus, and the beginning of the New Heaven and Earth and God's Kingdom, coincides with the resurrection of our Savior, Jesus.

<u>Is it what you expected?</u>

After hearing my entire life that the end of the world, as described in the Bible, was going to be catastrophic, it is to me, quite refreshing to finally realize that there will be no end to the life we all share on this planet.

His kingdom was established 2,000 years ago. Check out this passage found in ***Isaiah 9:6-7...***

For unto us a Child is born, Unto us a Son is given; And the government will be upon His shoulder. And His name will be called Wonderful, Counselor, Mighty God, Everlasting Father, Prince of Peace. Of the increase of His government and peace There will be no end, Upon the throne of David and over His kingdom, To order it and establish it with judgment and justice From that time forward, even forever. The zeal of the Lord of hosts will perform this.

And this one found in ***Luke 1:32-33...***

And behold, you will conceive in your womb and bring forth a Son, and shall call His name JESUS. He will be great, and will be called the Son of the Highest; and the Lord God will give Him the throne of His father David. And He will reign over the house of Jacob forever, and of His kingdom there will be no end."

I have found that most people do not believe God's kingdom has been established, because they are expecting a physical kingdom centered around the New Jerusalem. In fact, when sharing this idea with a CAM leader that I have always respected as a very intelligent man and Bible scholar, he laughed at me. He then went to another room and came back with a shoe box full of notes from his own studies. Among these notes were several renderings of what he expected the New Jerusalem to look like.

You see, he expected a physical city that he could see. Because he cannot see it with his eyes, he cannot accept that it is here already. Jesus covered this in ***Luke 17:20-21...***

Now when He was asked by the Pharisees when the kingdom of God would come, He answered them and said, "The kingdom of God does not come with observation; nor will they say, 'See here!' or 'See there!' For indeed, the kingdom of God is within you."

The word "observation", in this passage, means ocular evidence or evidence that can be seen with the eyes. That tells me that we will never "see" the kingdom. It is among us, just as we have shown you. In fact, the New Jerusalem is us. We are God's people. We are His kingdom. ***Matthew 16:28...***

Assuredly, I say to you, there are some standing here who shall not taste death till they see the Son of Man coming in His kingdom."

Jesus said this before He died, indicating that His kingdom was nearly here.

There are so many more things to show you. Forget about what you were taught, or what you were expecting, because Jesus is far greater than that. He did more than we ever thought possible. He did it in the hour we least expected.

The Hour We Least Expected

Chapter 5

Is Jesus Coming Back?

In chapter 4, we showed you that the end of the world, as described in the Bible, was actually just a symbolic reference to the end of the Old Covenant, or the Law. It was the end of the world, because it was the end of the way the world operated at that time. The "old order of things" passed away and the new order began with the resurrection of Jesus.

The CAM, or Currently Accepted Message, has a lot of ideas that are all interlocking. In other words, you cannot say the end of the world has happened without dealing with other doctrinal beliefs such as, "the second coming of Christ", "judgment day", "the rapture", "the resurrection of the dead", "the separation of the sheep and the goats", "the 70 weeks of Daniel" and the things Jesus said in Matthew 24 and Luke 17.

In this chapter, we will cover these ideas one at a time and show you how they each fit into our new belief.

Common Doctrines Not Found in the Bible

Several months before the completion of final revision of this book, we sent out a "test" copy to 30 people that we knew and trusted to give us an honest review. Some of these people were already in agreement with us, some were blind-sided with this information, and some we knew would be in total opposition to what we are saying.

One of my old friends, who still remains in total opposition to our message, pointed out a phrase that we had typed and noted that this phrase was not found anywhere in the Bible.

The phrase was "Jesus saved the entire world".

He is correct.

This phrase, with this exact wording, is not found in the Bible.

Does that mean that it is not true?

If so, then we believe that it is time to look at some phrases that we hear the CAM use daily that are nowhere to be found in the good book.

Where can one find "the age of accountability" in the Bible?

Or how about the "sinners prayer"?

The common word "rapture" is nowhere to be found.

Where does the Bible say that I must make Jesus my "Personal Lord and Savior"?

My point is that we have all heard these words and phrases used so much that we are shocked when we find out they are not in the Bible.

The Second Coming

Coincidentally, the phrase "second coming" is nowhere to be found in the Bible either. It is one of the most talked about events in the Christian world, but where is it mentioned in the Bible?

Like we said before, there are so many ideas stacked on top of each other in the CAM, we just cannot simply say that Jesus is not making another trip to planet Earth without dealing with all of them.

So for now, we will just say that some of the things that "scholars" believe will happen at the second coming of Jesus, already happened. They just happened in a way that we least expected and in the hour we least expected.

How could it be that we overlooked these things?

Well, the Bible is a mystery and mysteries take time to solve.

Let's move on to some of the sub-events that are supposed to coincide with the "second coming" and see if we can determine if they have happened yet.

Judgment Day

Judgment Day is a big deal.

If the CAM is right, there will be a day, in the near future, that Jesus will return to Earth and every one of us will stand before Him and be held accountable for everything we have done.

If they are correct, that Judgment Day is in the future, then we must say that we are 100% wrong about everything. Everyone cannot go to Heaven like we are suggesting, unless the Day of Judgment has already been accomplished.

We already pointed out some wording that Paul used in Romans that sounds like he believed the Judgment to be final. Check it out, ***Romans 5:18...***

Therefore, as through one man's offense judgment came to all men, resulting in condemnation, even so through one Man's righteous act the free gift came to all men, resulting in justification of life.

Paul is saying here that ALL of mankind was judged and condemned as a result of the actions and decision of Adam. Coincidentally, he is also suggesting that the choice of Jesus has reversed this effect on us.

Look what Jesus said about Judgment Day in ***John 5:19-29...***

Then Jesus answered and said to them, "Most assuredly, I say to you, the Son can do nothing of Himself, but what He sees the Father do; for whatever He does, the Son also does in like manner. For the Father loves the Son, and shows Him all things that He Himself does; and He will show Him greater works than these, that you may marvel. For as the Father raises the dead and gives life to them, even so the Son gives life to whom He will. For the Father judges no one, but has committed all judgment to the Son, that all should honor the Son just as they honor the Father. He who does not honor the Son does not honor the Father who sent Him. "Most assuredly, I say to you, he who hears My word and believes in Him who sent Me has everlasting life, and shall not come into judgment, but has passed from death into life. Most assuredly, I say to you, the hour is coming, and now is, when the dead will hear the voice of

the Son of God; and those who hear will live. For as the Father has life in Himself, so He has granted the Son to have life in Himself, and has given Him authority to execute judgment also, because He is the Son of Man. Do not marvel at this; for the hour is coming in which all who are in the graves will hear His voice and come forth— those who have done good, to the resurrection of life, and those who have done evil, to the resurrection of condemnation.

In this passage, Jesus says that God, the Father, has given Jesus the job of judging the world. Jesus then says that if anyone believes, then they will not come into the judgment. (Don't forget what we said in chapter 2 that nobody believed.) Then He says that He is going to judge us by our works, those who have done good, and those who have done evil.

The point of showing you this passage is that Jesus tells us that this hour is coming very soon.

Did He say these things in the 1980's?

No, He said this 2,000 years ago.

Does that mean that He is just a little slow?

No way!

I have learned that when something in the Bible doesn't fit my doctrine the way I think it should, then that is a good time to question my doctrine, rather than just forcing it to fit by saying that the verse doesn't mean what it says.

Now to one of my favorite passages… ***John 12:31-33...***

Now is the judgment of this world; now the ruler

of this world will be cast out. And I, if I am lifted up from the earth, will draw all peoples to Myself." This He said, signifying by what death He would die.

Here Jesus says that it is finally time for judgment.

He also says that if He is lifted up, He will draw ALL to Himself.

What does this tell us?

Verse 33 says that Jesus was talking about His death, so that tells me that the time for the judgment was at the cross.

Whether you are with me on this or not, just think about this for a bit.

The Bible says that when Jesus was on the cross, the sins of the entire world were placed on Him.

Jesus says in John 5 that at the time for judgment, He is going to judge us according to the Law. Sin or evil will be punished, and good (no sin) will be rewarded.

If Jesus took the sins of the world upon Him at the cross and then the judgment was determined at that moment, then Jesus would be punished for everyone's sins, while everyone else would be set free.

So does the Bible say that Jesus paid our penalty for sin?

Check out ***Hebrews 2:9...***

But we see Jesus, who was made a little lower than the angels, for the suffering of death crowned with glory and honor, that He, by the grace of God, might taste death for everyone.

It doesn't make any sense that Jesus would pay for the sins of the world before the world was judged. Everyone knows that a sentence is not given until the verdict is read.

Judgment Day was at the cross and Jesus paid our debt.

<u>The Rapture</u>

Probably one of the most bizarre and fanciful doctrines in the CAM is the idea that one of these days, ALL of the Christians are going to disappear, leaving the rest of the world in utter chaos.

Not all Christians believe this, but there are many CAM camps out there stating this future event to be a fact.

Many books and movies have been made about this fictitious event, and no doubt lots of money has been made from the sales of these books and movies.

If you are a believer in the rapture theory, then you are going to either be very upset when you read this, or very pleased when your fears are put to rest.

I did believe in this event for most of my life. As we said earlier in this book, we believed most everything our pastors and teachers told us. When a person gets on the platform at church and speaks with authority, people are apt to believe what they say.

Unfortunately, up until now, nobody has been able to tell them they are wrong, because they always have the argument that it just hasn't happened yet.

Now we are going to show you just where they get these ideas, and how they have so grossly misinterpreted a very simple text into a very imaginary event that will not happen.

Here is the text that is most commonly used to support the rapture doctrine… ***1Thess 4:13-18...***

But I do not want you to be ignorant, brethren, concerning those who have fallen asleep, lest you sorrow as others who have no hope. For if we believe that Jesus died and rose again, even so God will bring with Him those who sleep in Jesus. For this we say to you by the word of the Lord, that we who are alive and remain until the coming of the Lord will by no means precede those who are asleep. For the Lord Himself will descend from heaven with a shout, with the voice of an archangel, and with the trumpet of God. And the dead in Christ will rise first. Then we who are alive and remain shall be caught up together with them in the clouds to meet the Lord in the air. And thus we shall always be with the Lord. Therefore comfort one another with these words.

When the preacher in church explains this passage to a group of unquestioning people, it is easy to see his point of view.

According to most CAM teachers, this passage means that one day, there will be a sounding of a trumpet and then the dead will come out of their graves and then ALL those who believe in Jesus will disappear as He delivers them from this planet.

Obviously if this were true, then it would be a scary event for those who remain here afterwards.

For those of you who want a good laugh after you read our explanation of this passage, go to the internet and search "rapture videos". You will find quite a selection of video interpretations of this passage.

So let's look at this passage and see what it really means. Let's start with the subject first. Reread verse 13...

But I would not have you ignorant, brothers, concerning those who are asleep, that you be not grieved, even as others who have no hope.

My interpretation…

"Let me tell you about what happens to people when they die so you don't worry like those who do not have this information and therefore do not have the hope that you do"

Verse 14...

For if we believe that Jesus died and rose again, even so God will also bring with Him all those who have fallen asleep through Jesus.

Me…

"Because we believe that Jesus died and rose again, we also then believe that God also brought with Jesus those who were already dead"

Verse 15...

For we say this to you by the Word of the Lord, that we who are alive and remain until the coming of the Lord shall not go before those who are asleep.

Me...

"For we quote the Word when we say that we who were still alive when Jesus came are not going to go to be with Him before those who were already dead before He came"

Verse 16...

For the Lord Himself shall descend from Heaven with a shout, with the voice of the archangel and with the trumpet of God. And the dead in Christ shall rise first.

Still quoting from the Word, Paul says that the Word says that Jesus "shall descend"...

Many "scholars" will tell you that because it says "shall descend" makes this a future event, and we agree.

The problem with their theory is that they have failed to see that Paul was interpreting an old scripture when he wrote this. He was not saying that it "shall" happen, but that the Old Covenant said it "shall" happen. You must pair this verse with 15 to see that Paul is referring to prophecies of old when he was telling us how things work now.

Me...

"For the Word said that Jesus Himself shall descend from Heaven with a shout, with the voice of an archangel, and with the trump of God. And the dead in Christ will rise first."

I know some of you will say, "You see it says "in Christ" meaning only those who accepted Him."

But wait... we are talking about those who were dead before Christ ever came to earth.

They never had a chance to accept or reject Him, and we surely cannot say that their status was dependent upon their actions, or there would be no one set free. The Bible makes it very clear that... Rom 3:10 "There is none righteous, no not one". And then Paul repeats this in Rom 3:20 "because by the works of the Law none of all flesh will be justified in His sight; for through the Law *is* the knowledge of sin." So their "in Christ" status cannot be dependent upon their ability to keep the law.

As we have seen in previous chapters of this book, ALL were in Christ when He died. ALL were drawn to Him upon the cross and were raised with Him at the resurrection.

Verse 17...

Then we who are alive and remain shall be caught up together with them in the clouds, to meet the Lord in the air. And so we shall ever be with the Lord.

Me…

"Then we who are still alive when this happens shall be caught up together with them in the clouds (when we die), to meet the Lord in the air. And so we shall ever be with the Lord."

You have to add the words "when we die" because that is the subject of the paragraph.

Paul is simply explaining how death works now that the Lord has come and finished His work.

Verse 18...

Therefore comfort one another with these words.

Here is another clue.

What about the rapture theory is comforting?

It would take a very selfish evil person to find comfort in the idea that the people left behind on earth will be in total chaos after a large number of people vanish?

Obviously Paul is not describing any such idea, or surely he would have elaborated a little longer.

Re-read this passage over and over until you see that Paul was simply describing what happens to people when they die. Before Jesus came, those who "fell asleep" went to a place called "shehole" to await the Judgment Day, when their final destination would be determined.

In the next chapter of this book, you will find further explanation of this, but here Paul is explaining that things have changed since Jesus rose from the dead and that we can have peace regarding our brothers who have passed.

In the Twinkling of an Eye

Most CAM members will tell you that one day in the future, Jesus is going to swing by and pick them up and leave the rest of the World in utter chaos.

They get this idea from a few Bible passages including this one… ***1Corinthians 15: 51-52...***

Behold, I tell you a mystery: We shall not all sleep, but we shall all be changed—in a moment, in the twinkling of an eye, at the last trumpet. For the trumpet will sound, and the dead will be raised incorruptible, and we shall be changed.

One of the flaws in this idea is that they have failed to realize that ALL of mankind did change in the twinkling of an eye.

Do you remember what happened to the veil in the temple when Jesus died? ***Matthew 27:51...***

Then, behold, the veil of the temple was torn in two from top to bottom; and the earth quaked, and the rocks were split,

The significance of this is that this veil served a very big purpose.

It was the barrier that protected the priests from the power of God that was behind the curtain, coming from the Ark of the Covenant.

The stone tablets from the First Covenant were inside this golden box.

If the priests were to go into the room that contained the Ark, without the proper preparations, they would die.

So why did they not die when the curtain ripped, exposing them to the Ark?

It is because when Jesus died, ALL of mankind was changed.

The Ark did not have any power over us anymore because it was symbolic of the Old Covenant that was contained inside.

The truth is simple…

There is a New Covenant now and it is contained inside of us!!! It was prophesied in ***Jeremiah 31:31-34...***

Behold, the days are coming, says the LORD, when I will make a new covenant with the house of Israel and with the house of Judah—not according to the covenant that I made with their fathers in the day that I took them by the hand to lead them out of the land of Egypt, My covenant which they broke, though I was a husband to them, says the LORD. But this is the covenant that I will make with the house of Israel after those days, says the LORD: I will put My law in their minds, and write it on their hearts; and I will be their God, and they shall be My people. No more shall every man teach his neighbor, and every man his brother, saying, 'Know the LORD,' for they all shall know Me, from the least of them to the greatest of them, says the LORD. For I will forgive their iniquity, and their sin I will remember no more."

When did this happen?

CAM leaders will tell you to expect this to happen in some future hour.

The ironic thing is that Jesus said that it would happen in The Hour We Least Expected!!!

The other passage in the Bible that Christians claim is about the rapture is found in 1Corinthians 15:51-52...

Behold, I tell you a mystery: We shall not all sleep, but we shall all be changed— in a moment, in the twinkling of an eye, at the last trumpet. For the trumpet will sound, and the dead will be raised incorruptible, and we shall be changed.

Once again, Paul is merely discussing death.

Read the entire chapter carefully and you will see that it is about what happens to people upon death, but for some reason these 2 verses are made out to be about a crazy event that will leave the world in chaos.

Paul is merely explaining a mystery to us.

What happens to people when they die?

Paul here says that "we shall not all fall asleep". He is referring to the way it used to be before Jesus came. When someone died, they went to a holding cell called "shehole" or "hades" to wait for the coming of the one who would set them free. They were those captives, asleep in the grave.

Paul says that this is no longer how it works. At the moment that the trumpet sounds (the cross and resurrection), we will all be changed (because everything changed).

The Resurrection of the Dead

Now many CAM members will tell you that the dead have not risen yet and are still "asleep" waiting for Judgment Day, but look at what Jesus says here in ***John 5:25…***

Most assuredly, I say to you, the hour is coming, and now is, when the dead will hear the voice of the Son of God; and those who hear will live.

Look how He says "the hour is coming <u>and now is</u>". He was saying that this time was just about to happen, 2,000 years ago.

What better time for the dead to hear His voice than when He makes His visit to Sheole/Hades (when He dies) to set the captives free?

Many preachers will tell you that when Jesus died, He at least visited the dead and took some of them with Him.

Why wouldn't He take them all?

Is it possible that He went to Sheole and took an altar call and some didn't want to go with Him?

They were already dead!!!

Who there wouldn't go?

This makes no sense.

When Jesus died, we were ALL found guilty, but rather than face eternal death, He took our place and tasted death for all.

When He rose again, ALL who were dead rose also and went to be with Him forever.

Back to 1Corinthians 15 MKJV for more proof... ***Verses 12-20...***

But if Christ is proclaimed, that He was raised from the dead, how do some among you say that there is no resurrection of the dead? But if there is no resurrection of the dead, neither has Christ been raised. And if Christ has not been raised, then our proclamation

is worthless, and your faith is also worthless. And we are also found to be false witnesses of God, <u>because we testified of God that He raised Christ; whom He did not raise if the dead are not raised. For if the dead are not raised, then Christ is not raised.</u> And if Christ is not raised, your faith is foolish; you are yet in your sins. Then also those that fell asleep in Christ were lost. If in this life only we have hope in Christ, we are of all men most miserable. But now Christ has risen from the dead, and has become the firstfruit of those who slept.

Notice that the writer says "Christ has risen from *the* dead, *and* has become the firstfruit of those who slept."

Slept!!

Past tense!!

Christ rose from the dead, and so did ALL who were dead.

This whole passage of 1Corinthians 15 is explaining that the dead have been raised. Read the underlined section from above again and notice that the writer is stating that the resurrection of Christ and of the dead is a simultaneous and combined event.

In other words, you cannot have one without the other.

Now look at the next 2 verses. ***Verses 21-22...***

For since death is through man, the resurrection of the dead also is through a Man. For as in Adam all die, even so in Christ all will be made alive.

As in Adam, ALL died, so in Christ ALL are made alive!!!

How much simpler can it be?

Verse 23...

But each in his own order: Christ the first-fruit, and afterward they who are Christ's at His coming;

Paul says that it will happen in this order, Christ first, then those who were already dead when He came. ***Verses 24-26...***

then is the end, when He delivers the kingdom to God, even the Father; when He makes to cease all rule and all authority and power. for it is right for Him to reign until He has put all the enemies under His feet. The last enemy made to cease is death.

"Then is the end."

Many will say "see here he says the end isn't here yet".

That's not what he is saying. Paul is telling us how it was going to happen. He says that Jesus would be here until He put all the enemies under His feet, the last one being death.

Then look what he says next in ***verse 27...***

For He put all things under His feet. But when He says that all things have been put under His feet, it is plain that it excepts Him who has put all things under Him.

He said the end will be when Jesus put His enemies under His feet, and the last enemy is death. Then Paul said Jesus DID put all things under His feet. That means it is over.

Jesus put death under His feet when He rose from the dead.

(To reiterate an earlier point, let's look at ***Revelation 20:13-***

And the sea gave up the dead in it. And death and hell delivered up the dead in them. And each one of them was judged according to their works. And death and hell (hades) were cast into the Lake of Fire. This is the second death.

As discussed before, the book of Revelation has been taught as containing future events, however we have demonstrated how that Jesus, through His death and His resurrection, has defeated death.

Here in Revelation we see this event from a different angle.

The dead were released and judged against the law, as Jesus said would happen in ***John 5:28-29***

Do not marvel at this, for the hour is coming in which all who are in the graves shall hear His voice, and shall come forth, those who have done good to the resurrection of life, and those who have practiced evil to the resurrection of condemnation.

So to tie this all together, according to the passage in 1Corinthians 15, Jesus has indeed defeated death, which is shown here again from a different perspective in Revelation 20.

This also demonstrates that the judgment of the dead, that Jesus said was about to happen in John 5, is the same event described in Revelation 20.

Once more, this also demonstrated that Hades itself, that is the world of the dead, has been destroyed as well in the same fire judgment that we will be discussing further in chapter 5.

The point is that this has all already happened, it just happened in a way that we least expected.

That sums up the rapture and the resurrection of the dead. Not one of the verses that the CAM uses to explain this event is used correctly.

These verses are all simply explaining death and how things work now that Jesus has put death under his feet.

Death has been destroyed.

The 70 Weeks of Daniel

I have mentioned the 70 weeks of Daniel to many people in the last few years, and it seems that most average Christians or church goers do not know much about this Old Testament prophecy, but I understand that I cannot possibly say that the end has come without explaining the 70 weeks of Daniel.

This is a very technical passage of scripture and a mystery that thousands have tried to solve.

We will now add our name to the list of people who have a theory as to what this passage is all about.

Let's look at the text, ***Daniel 9:24-27...***

"Seventy weeks are determined For your people and for your holy city, To finish the transgression, To make an end of sins, To make reconciliation for iniquity, To bring in everlasting righteousness, To seal up vision and prophecy, And to anoint the Most Holy. "Know therefore and understand, That from the going forth of the command To restore and build Jerusalem Until Messiah the Prince, There shall be seven weeks and sixty-two weeks; The street shall be built again, and the

wall, Even in troublesome times. "And after the sixty-two weeks Messiah shall be cut off, but not for Himself; And the people of the prince who is to come Shall destroy the city and the sanctuary. The end of it shall be with a flood, And till the end of the war desolations are determined. Then he shall confirm a covenant with many for one week; But in the middle of the week He shall bring an end to sacrifice and offering. And on the wing of abominations shall be one who makes desolate, Even until the consummation, which is determined, Is poured out on the desolate."

This prophecy was given to Daniel, giving us clues to when the end would come. It says that it will take 70 weeks to accomplish these things:

1. to finish the transgression
2. to make an end of sins
3. to make reconciliation for iniquity
4. to bring in everlasting righteousness
5. seal up the vision and prophecy
6. to anoint the Most Holy

Most theories, regarding this prophecy, put this as a future event.

CAM leaders will tell you that this event could not have happened because of the six things that were supposed to be accomplished have not been accomplished.

By now, I hope you can see that we have already made a case for each of these details, but we will quickly review them.

1. to finish the transgression

Transgression in this passage means “a revolt”. It is describing the rebellion of God’s people against the Law since no one has been able to keep it. Obviously the revolt is over since we are forgiven and the Law has been made obsolete.

2. to make an end of sins

As we have already pointed out, sin is to transgress or break the Law. When Jesus died, the Law died too. There is no longer any written definition of sin, therefore sin, by definition, is over.

3. to make reconciliation for iniquity

If Jesus did not make reconciliation for iniquity, then what did He do?

4. to bring in everlasting righteousness

When Jesus died and rose again, He revealed His righteousness which does not come by keeping the Law, but simply because of His grace.

It is simple.

He wanted to forgive you, so He did and He did it forever.

5. seal up the vision and prophecy

As we pointed out in chapter 4, when Jesus said "it is finished", it was. All Bible prophecy was fulfilled with the death and resurrection of Jesus. ***Matthew 5:18...***

For assuredly, I say to you, till heaven and earth pass away, one jot or one tittle will by no means pass from the law till all is fulfilled.

When Jesus died, the Law died also which, according to this

verse, means that heaven and earth passed away and ALL things have been accomplished.

6. to anoint the Most Holy

In John 12, Jesus says that it was finally time for Him to be glorified. Jesus is the Most Holy Messiah, and the event that makes Him the Messiah is the cross and resurrection.

The Gap Theory

According to the prophecy, there is a period of time that has been specifically planned to accomplish those 6 things. That period of time is 70 weeks.

It is very important that we point out that the Hebrew word that was translated into the English word "weeks" means "sevened". This word can mean 7 days, 7 months, or 7 years.

Many CAM leaders will insist that it only means 7 years, but consider this passage of scripture found in the very next chapter. ***Daniel 10:2-3...***

In those days I, Daniel, was mourning three full weeks. I ate no pleasant food, no meat or wine came into my mouth, nor did I anoint myself at all, till three whole weeks were fulfilled.

Daniel surely doesn't mean that he did not eat for 21 years. There are plenty of other passages, in the Old Testament, that include this word, and it is easy to see that sometimes it is referring to days and sometimes years.

The prophecy says that the weeks are divided into 7 weeks, 62 weeks, and then one final week.

Like we said, the timing of this prophecy is a huge mystery.

Many theories have been derived from many different dates and mathematical methods. In order to save trees, we will not go into all of the different ones, but simply share the one that makes sense to us.

What we believe to be the most popular and accurate theory places the first 69 weeks as ending on the day Jesus rode into town on the colt. This makes sense to us because of the following passage, ***Luke 19:35-40…***

Then they brought him to Jesus. And they threw their own clothes on the colt, and they set Jesus on him. And as He went, many spread their clothes on the road. Then, as He was now drawing near the descent of the Mount of Olives, the whole multitude of the disciples began to rejoice and praise God with a loud voice for all the mighty works they had seen, saying: " 'BLESSED IS THE KING WHO COMES IN THE NAME OF THE LORD!' Peace in heaven and glory in the highest!" And some of the Pharisees called to Him from the crowd, "Teacher, rebuke Your disciples." But He answered and said to them, "I tell you that if these should keep silent, the stones would immediately cry out."

This day was prophesied and if the people did not declare Him the Messiah, He says the rocks would have cried out.

This is significant because this was the last day of the 69th week of years.

The prophecy says that the 69th week will end on the day that the Messiah comes and this is the day that Jesus was officially declared the Messiah.

The gap theory suggests that the last "week" has not happened yet, so there is a gap between the 69th and 70th week.

Many believe this last week is a week of years like the others obviously are, however, because of the way the weeks are divided, it is possible that this last week could be any size week, including a week of days.

Several times I have asked pastors and other teachers if this is possible, and although no one has told me that it was not, they all seem to agree that it would be very inconsistent to change the last week to days when the others are years.

Although I agree that it may appear inconsistent, I still cannot find how this inconsistency is relevant.

Also, doesn't it seem very inconsistent that the first 69 weeks were consecutive and the last one happens thousands of years later?

I mean if God is going to make it work out to the very day, why would he then leave a gap between the 69th and the 70th ?

Also, no one seems to think it is odd that one of the biggest prophecies in the Bible given by the Messianic Angel, Gabriel, who always spoke of Jesus, leaves the biggest climactic event of the Bible, (the cross and resurrection), in the gap?

That would mean that the cross and resurrection have nothing to do with the fulfilling of this prophecy!

Most of the CAM will say that the very event that makes Jesus the Messiah actually happens outside of the context of the 70 weeks prophecy in which the very subject of the prophecy IS the Messiah Himself!

This seems very inconsistent to me, especially since Jesus said that the Law and the Prophets were always referring to Him.

You cannot possibly leave the most pivotal and most important and defining event in all of human history, that is the event that defines Jesus as our Messiah, in a gap outside of the timeline of the 70 weeks prophecy!

That is an absolutely absurd idea!

Let's move on…

Perfect Timing

This is our theory on the timing of the 70th week.

The first 69 weeks were of years and they ended with the triumphant entry of Christ on Saturday.

The next day was Sunday.

It was day 1 of the final week of days.

Monday was day 2.

Tuesday was day 3.

Wednesday was day 4 and Jesus was hung on the cross where He died at the ninth hour (½ way through the day). (Although tradition places Jesus death on a Friday, it is now widely accepted that it was on Wednesday.)

Thursday was day 5.

Friday was day 6.

And Saturday was day 7.

At the beginning of day 8, Sunday, Mary discovered the

empty tomb, meaning that Jesus had risen just before the beginning of the 8th day, or at the end of the 7th day.

This makes 7 days exactly, with His death exactly in the middle.

Then he shall confirm a covenant with many for one week; But in the middle of the week He shall bring an end to sacrifice and offering. And on the wing of abominations shall be one who makes desolate, Even until the consummation, which is determined, Is poured out on the desolate."

In the midst of the week, Jesus became the ultimate sacrifice and offering, therefore ending God's recognition of any future animal sacrifices.

This also correlates with what Jesus said about this period of time as found in ***Matthew 24:22...***

And unless those days should be shortened, no flesh would be saved. But for the elect's sake, those days shall be shortened.

You see, the last week of the seventy weeks prophecy was cut or divided or made special and different from the other weeks.

The first were sixty nine weeks of years, but in keeping with the details of the prophecy and making both the days of the tribulation shortened and maintaining the definition of the word "week" God chose to make this last "week" a week of days.

When this timeline is considered and superimposed on top of the details found in this and related prophecies, I see nothing more than the absolute clearest picture I have yet to see concerning the event.

This explanation deals with all of the details that couldn't be explained through the foundational point of view of the CAM.

So what about the destruction of the city and sanctuary or temple? Remember when Jesus said this in ***John 2:19...***

Jesus answered and said to them, "Destroy this temple, and in three days I will raise it up."

Jesus was the sanctuary.

Mankind was the city.

When Jesus died, ALL of mankind "died".

Remember what we said earlier about how God often spoke to "Jerusalem" in the Old Testament? "Jerusalem" was symbolic of the people of God. When Jesus died, they died. When Jesus rose again, ALL of mankind was made New!!!

When "***the people of the prince who is to come***", (God's people, the Jews), killed Jesus on the cross, they did not realize they were fulfilling the prophecy of Daniel by destroying the "sanctuary" (Jesus) and the "city" (God's people).

One Or Two Princes?

CAM teachers will also use this prophecy to lend credibility to their theory that the "Anti-Christ is going to come into power in the near future.

Their reason for this is the mentioning of two Princes in the prophecy.

In verse 25, it says "Messiah the Prince" and in verse 26, it says "And the people of the prince who shall come".

They are both the same Hebrew word "nagiyd". The argument that these are two different princes is made by many because of two main reasons.

One is that the first one says "Messiah the Prince" and the other just says "prince", and therefore cannot be the same prince.

The other reason is that the second one says "the prince who shall come" and therefore means that this one is coming later.

I have read this passage over and over and I no longer see the relevance of either of these two arguments.

First of all, if Daniel wrote "Messiah, the Prince", just one sentence before writing "the prince", is it not possible that he felt no reason to reconfirm it was the same one?

For example, if I said "Justin, my friend, is coming over for dinner", and then said "My friend is bringing dessert"; nobody would argue that the second "friend" is Justin.

Secondly, to say that because the second "prince" was "to come" is also irrelevant, because the prophecy is also saying that the first "prince" wasn't here yet either, so they both are "to come".

A simple understanding of language can make it quite possible and most likely that these two "princes" are the same.

It is Finished

The 70 weeks of Daniel were concluded with the week of the cross and resurrection of Jesus and the timing is perfect.

God confirmed His New Covenant to us during this week, just as the prophecy states.

This is the same covenant that Jeremiah wrote about in Jeremiah 31:31-34.

There is not a 3rd Covenant coming.

It is finished!!!

Matthew 24

Matthew 24 is a very big chapter for those discussing the end times. In this chapter, Jesus says many things that have puzzled people for years.

Of course the most commonly accepted theory regarding the prophecies in this chapter is that they still have not happened.

I will point out some of the most obvious flaws in the theory that marks this prophecy unfulfilled.

Here is the text and my commentary as we go…***Matthew 24:1-2...***

Then Jesus went out and departed from the temple, and His disciples came up to show Him the buildings of the temple. And Jesus said to them, "Do you not see all these things? Assuredly, I say to you, not one stone shall be left here upon another, that shall not be thrown down."

Remember the verse we just read above where Jesus said that He would rebuild the temple in three days?

Many scholars suggest that Matt 24:2 is fulfilled in 70AD when the Romans attacked Jerusalem and left it in shambles.

The biggest reason that I have a problem with this theory is that Jesus states here that "***not one stone shall be left here upon another, that shall not be thrown down***."

There still remains to this day, 2,000 years later, a wall called "the wailing wall". It is kept by the Jews in remembrance of the temple that was destroyed in 70AD. Although the physical temple was destroyed, it does not fulfill the prophecy spoken by Jesus here in Matt 24:2 because He said "***not one stone shall be left here upon another, that shall not be thrown down***." The remaining of this wall renders that theory incorrect.

So what then was He referring to?

I believe this teaching in Matt 24 is like every other teaching of Jesus in that it is symbolic.

Jesus always taught with symbolism, making the true meanings of His stories a mystery to be deciphered. So again, I see this as another symbol of the destruction of the Old Jerusalem that took place symbolically when Jesus died at the cross, just as we mentioned in the segment of the 70 weeks of Daniel. Jesus was the "temple" and His people, the "city".

Matthew 24:3...

Now as He sat on the Mount of Olives, the disciples came to Him privately, saying, "Tell us, when will these things be? And what will be the sign of Your coming, and of the end of the age?"

And the CAM still asks today.

Remember what we wrote in chapter 4, that Jesus could not have explained the end if He had not been given the Revelation. Note Revelations 1:1...

The Revelation of Jesus Christ, which God gave Him to show His servants—things which must shortly take place. And He sent and signified it by His angel to His servant John,

God gave this Revelation to Jesus, so He could show His servants (the disciples) what was going to happen.

In Matthew 24, Jesus quotes things that are written in the Revelation.

How could He have done this when Revelation was not written by John until several decades later?

verse 4-6...

And Jesus answered and said to them: "Take heed that no one deceives you. For many will come in My name, saying, 'I am the Christ,' and will deceive many. And you will hear of wars and rumors of wars. See that you are not troubled; for all these things must come to pass, but the end is not yet.

"***but the end is not yet***"

Many people use modern day events to suggest that the end is coming, but here Jesus says that these things DO NOT mark the end. ***Verse 7-12...***

For nation will rise against nation, and kingdom

against kingdom. And there will be famines, pestilences, and earthquakes in various places. All these are the beginning of sorrows. "Then they will deliver you up to tribulation and kill you, and you will be hated by all nations for My name's sake. And then many will be offended, will betray one another, and will hate one another. Then many false prophets will rise up and deceive many. And because lawlessness will abound, the love of many will grow cold.

Although I understand why many think these things sound like events of today, they were also true of the time when Jesus was here. Wars, earthquakes, famines, false prophets, all happened back then.

Verses 13-14...

But he who endures to the end shall be saved. And this gospel of the kingdom will be preached in all the world as a witness to all the nations, and then the end will come.

Here is a very large stumbling block for many CAM members.

Because it is still tradition to see the need to accept Jesus in order to receive the grace He provided, many see the "gospel" as not having reached the whole world, but further study of these words will reveal that "the world" meant the Roman empire, and "the gospel of the kingdom" is **<u>not</u>** the Good News of Christ's victory, but rather the proclamation that "the kingdom of God is at hand" which was accomplished by John the Baptist and the sending out of the disciples into the various cities of the Roman empire prior to Christ's crucifixion.

Verse 15...

"Therefore when you see the 'ABOMINATION OF DESOLATION,' spoken of by Daniel the prophet, standing in the holy place" (whoever reads, let him understand),

The fact that the writer says "whoever reads, let him understand" is a clue that this statement given to us by Christ is a clue or a hint of something deeper going on.

Just like Christ referred to the temple but was really talking about Himself, I believe that the abomination of desolation is also symbolic of what happened to Christ during His death.

Verse 24 in this passage explains that the tribulation of this time would be greater than anything before this time until then, nor would it ever be this bad again afterwards.

I believe that the abomination, or the filthy and detestable thing, is the sin of the entire world that was taken on by the purest being that ever walked the planet.

The filthy and detestable was put on the purest and most holy One and He carried this burden, this judgment, and the wrath that followed it.

As we have mentioned before, this is the "Big Switch" which was the most unexpected event in human history.

The wrath and judgment was on its way to all of mankind, just as Jesus and many others before Him had prophesied, however, He chose to step in and take upon Himself the abomination, that is the sin of the entire world, and thus declaring Himself to be the only one deserving of the punishment and wrath that befell Him.

I can only begin to try to imagine what that must have looked like behind the scenes.

What does the spirit of Jesus look like as His perfection is mixed with all that is imperfect?

What did He feel?

There was such a major contrast happening inside of Him, it must have been awful.

As His father looked down on Him during this time, what did He see?

For a moment, even God Himself had a hard time dealing with this situation and briefly turned His head, but He remained with Jesus still the same.

He who hears needs to understand that this was THE event in which the unconditional love of the creator was demonstrated and proven.

Verses 16-20...

"then let those who are in Judea flee to the mountains. Let him who is on the housetop not go down to take anything out of his house. And let him who is in the field not go back to get his clothes. But woe to those who are pregnant and to those who are nursing babies in those days! And pray that your flight may not be in winter or on the Sabbath.

This passage is symbolic of the fear of the pouring out of the wrath of God that thankfully was taken on by Jesus instead of being poured on those who deserved it, mankind.

Verse 21...

For then there will be great tribulation, such as has not been since the beginning of the world until this time, no, nor ever shall be.

The wording of this sentence is peculiar. "***since the beginning of the world until this time, no, nor ever shall be***." If Jesus is talking about "the end" of something, why does He make this period of tribulation in the middle of this sentence?

In other words, by saying "from the beginning until now, nor any time after this", implies that this time was very close at hand and that this distress would not be repeated any time after this.

So what about the distress?

Again, I say that because Jesus endured the wrath of God for us, He alone experienced this great tribulation on the cross.

Verse 22...

And unless those days were shortened, no flesh would be saved; but for the elect's sake those days will be shortened.

Yes, the terrible events were shortened from a 7 year period, down to a 7 day period, and thankfully taken on by Christ, Himself.

This verse also this gives credibility to my theory that Daniel's 70th week was not of years but of days, making the expected time much shorter.

Verses 23-27...

Then if anyone says to you, 'Look, here is the Christ!' or 'There!' do not believe it. For false christs and false prophets will rise and show great signs and wonders to deceive, if possible, even the elect. See, I have told you beforehand. "Therefore if they say to you, 'Look, He is in the desert!' do not go out; or 'Look, He is in the inner rooms!' do not believe it. For as the lightning comes from the east and flashes to the west, so also will the coming of the Son of Man be.

Jesus day was as a bolt of lightning, it was quick and over before anyone even knew what happened. Even to this day, we are still working on solving the mystery of what actually happened.

Verse 28...

For wherever the carcass is, there the eagles will be gathered together.

This is obviously more symbolism. This time a carcass, or dead body, is referring to His death on the cross. We (the eagles) were drawn into His dead body, (if one died for all, then all died).

Check out this verse in ***Isaiah 26:19...***

Your dead shall live; <u>Together with my dead body they shall arise</u>. Awake and sing, you who dwell in dust; For your dew is like the dew of herbs, And the earth shall cast out the dead.

This passage is further proof to support our claim that when Jesus died, ALL died. We were drawn, symbolically, into Jesus body when He died, because He was our representative.

Verse 29…

"Immediately after the tribulation of those days the sun will be darkened, and the moon will not give its light; the stars will fall from heaven, and the powers of the heavens will be shaken.

Remember, the sun was dark for three hours and there was a great earthquake when Jesus was dying on the cross, (Matthew 27:51-53).

The phrase, "the stars shall fall from the heaven", is repeated symbolism in Rev 13 when the dragon slapped 1/3 of the stars from the sky with his tail.

This event was mentioned by Jesus in John 12:31. Jesus said it was time for the prince of this world to be cast down, referring to Satan's defeat at the cross. So the dragon, (Satan), was cast down and the heavenly bodies, (Satan's angels), were taken down with him.

Verse 30…

Then the sign of the Son of Man will appear in heaven, and then all the tribes of the earth will mourn, and they will see the Son of Man coming on the clouds of heaven with power and great glory.

The sign of Jesus is the cross and it appeared in the sky as Jesus was lifted up on it finishing the work He had come to do and it was with great power and glory that He did it.

Verse 31…

And He will send His angels with a great sound of a trumpet, and they will gather together His elect

from the four winds, from one end of heaven to the other.

This is more symbolism.

Although there is no record of anybody audibly hearing a trumpet, and it was probably very quiet when the cross was lifted, the cross of Jesus still, to this day, resounds around the world.

Verses 32-34...

"Now learn this parable from the fig tree: When its branch has already become tender and puts forth leaves, you know that summer is near. So you also, when you see all these things, know that it is near—at the doors! Assuredly, I say to you, this generation will by no means pass away till all these things take place.

Here is a huge key verse… "***this generation will by no means pass away till all these things take place***" Many Bible teachers explain this away by saying that since these things didn't happen, then it will be the generation that sees these things happen that will not pass. They only say this because they don't understand that these things did happen.

Look at what Jesus said in ***Luke 9:27...***

But I tell you truly, there are some standing here who shall not taste death till they see the kingdom of God."

Obviously, this means that the kingdom of God was not 2,000 years away from being established.

Verses 35-39...

Heaven and earth will pass away, but My words will by no means pass away. "But of that day and hour no one knows, not even the angels of heaven, but My Father only. But as the days of Noah were, so also will the coming of the Son of Man be. For as in the days before the flood, they were eating and drinking, marrying and giving in marriage, until the day that Noah entered the ark, and did not know until the flood came and took them all away, so also will the coming of the Son of Man be.

Heaven and Earth, the old order of things as mentioned in Revelation 21, passed away when Jesus died on the cross. As we have said before, this is symbolic of the passing of the Law or Old Covenant.

Nobody knew what was happening until it was over, and even then it is taking a long time to recognize just what happened because it happened in a way we least expected.

Verses 40-44...

Then two men will be in the field: one will be taken and the other left. Two women will be grinding at the mill: one will be taken and the other left. Watch therefore, for you do not know what hour your Lord is coming. But know this, that if the master of the house had known what hour the thief would come, he would have watched and not allowed his house to be broken into. Therefore you also be ready, for the Son of Man is coming at an hour you do not expect.

The taking of one and leaving the other is symbolic of the separation of us from our sins as also described as the separation of the sheep and goats or the wheat and tares in other various parables of Jesus. These parables are explained further in detail in chapter 6 of this book.

What physically appeared to be Jesus defeat (***an hour you do not expect***) was in fact His finest hour.

No one, at the time, believed that Jesus won the battle when He was hanging there, bloody, beaten, naked, and dying on a cross.

This was the least expected time to count as a victory.

Once again this is our claim and the driving point behind this book.

The Hour We Least Expected is the most unlikely hour in which it would seem that God had achieved the ultimate victory over sin.

However, after stepping back away from looking at one verse at a time and examining the whole of the Bible, it becomes increasingly clear that everything in the entire Bible points to this time Jesus spent on the cross, as being the climax in the ultimate story of true, unconditional love

Verses 45-51...

"Who then is a faithful and wise servant, whom his master made ruler over his household, to give them food in due season? Blessed is that servant whom his master, when he comes, will find so doing. Assuredly, I say to you that he will make him ruler over all his goods. But if that evil servant says in his heart, 'My master is delaying his coming,' and begins to beat his fellow servants, and to eat and drink with the drunkards, the master of that servant will come on a day when he is not looking for him and at an hour that he is not aware of,

and will cut him in two and appoint him his portion with the hypocrites. There shall be weeping and gnashing of teeth.

I believe this last passage symbolizes the grief that comes to those who do not understand that Jesus was 100% victorious.

Many Christians today are grief stricken due to the belief that millions of people will live in hell forever and that Jesus work was not finished while He was here.

Notice the line ***'My master is delaying his coming,'.***

We find this passage very ironic, considering the fact that so many do believe that the Master has delayed His final work.

The Hour We Least Expected

For thousands of years, the world expected a Messiah…
Isaiah 53...

Who has believed our report? And to whom has the arm of the LORD been revealed? For He shall grow up before Him as a tender plant, And as a root out of dry ground. He has no form or comeliness; And when we see Him, There is no beauty that we should desire Him. He is despised and rejected by men, A Man of sorrows and acquainted with grief. And we hid, as it were, our faces from Him; He was despised, and we did not esteem Him. Surely He has borne our griefs And carried our sorrows; Yet we esteemed Him stricken, Smitten by God, and afflicted. But He was wounded for our transgressions, He was bruised for our iniquities; The chastisement for our peace was upon Him, And by His stripes we are healed. All we like sheep have gone astray; We have turned, every one, to his own way; And the LORD has laid on Him the iniquity of us all. He was

oppressed and He was afflicted, Yet He opened not His mouth; He was led as a lamb to the slaughter, And as a sheep before its shearers is silent, So He opened not His mouth. He was taken from prison and from judgment, And who will declare His generation? For He was cut off from the land of the living; For the transgressions of My people He was stricken. And they made His grave with the wicked— But with the rich at His death, Because He had done no violence, Nor was any deceit in His mouth. Yet it pleased the LORD to bruise Him; He has put Him to grief. When You make His soul an offering for sin, He shall see His seed, He shall prolong His days, And the pleasure of the LORD shall prosper in His hand. He shall see the labor of His soul, and be satisfied. By His knowledge My righteous Servant shall justify many, For He shall bear their iniquities. Therefore I will divide Him a portion with the great, And He shall divide the spoil with the strong, Because He poured out His soul unto death, And He was numbered with the transgressors, And He bore the sin of many, And made intercession for the transgressors.

Jesus was NOT the Messiah that mankind expected.

He was not attractive. He was not rich. He did not wear a crown or command huge armies. His birthplace was a cold manger. He was from a small town.

Nothing about Him said "Prince", yet He spoke with authority and baffled even the wisest of leaders. He taught many things that had the sound of glory, yet as they all watched Him take His last breath, glory was not what they were thinking.

Jesus time on the cross appeared to be defeat. It was quiet and lowly, even embarrassing. But as is God's way, He chose this seemingly sad moment to be the hour in which He would save the World.

The World still doesn't believe He did it, but when He cried "It is finished", it was, and it all happened in the hour we least expected.

THE HOUR WE LEAST EXPECTED

CHAPTER 6

SO WHAT ABOUT HELL?

The Hour We ALL Dread

Imagine you are lying in your bed and your family is all gathered around visiting.

Your daughter is sharing with everyone the story about the time that you took her to get her first pet.

Everyone is laughing at her funny story and nodding their heads in agreement as if to confirm that the story fits the character of the person they have loved their whole life.

As the laughter ends, she hands you a card that reads "To My Dad".

The letter inside is long and beautiful and rich.

As you read the words, there is silence.

The smiling faces around you are suddenly wet with streams of love and heartache flowing down until they are absorbed by the soft white tissues they all brought in their pockets.

As you finish the letter and place it on your lap you can't speak. Instead you look each one in their eyes and nod.

There is no need for words anyway, because they already know.

You love them and they love you.

With the long release of a deep breath, your reality fades to a different scene.

Before the Judge

Suddenly you are standing in a large auditorium with what seems like a spotlight right in your face.

As a large book is opened in front of you, your knees begin to shake.

Your peaceful nature is overcome with fear and anxiety.

The figure in front of you shakes His head in disappointment as if to confirm that what He was looking for cannot be found.

Suddenly, on what looks like a thousand video screens, you recognize the video that is playing.

Scene after scene, every detail of your life is played in a very fast but chronological order.

There you are at your first day of school, then your high school graduation where you gave your big speech, then the birth of your kids.

Various moments of your life pass by quickly on the screens

until all of a sudden the video slows way down.

You are puzzled because you don't even recognize the scene.

Very confused, you continue to watch the video of yourself in your recliner flipping through the channels on your new television.

Then the doorbell rings and you get up to answer it. Very quickly you dismiss the gentlemen at the door and the video is paused.

Every eye in the room turns from the video to you.

Then a very deep voice asks you if you remember who those people were.

Quivering, you answer, "Yes… They were from the church just down the street. They were inviting me to church and I said no."

The silence is overtaken by the whispering of thousands as they can't help but discuss the situation.

"SILENCE!!!" the figure says.

You continue by explaining that you just never believed in supernatural things, especially the idea that an all-powerful being had hand formed you and all things that existed.

Humbly you ask the figure "Was I wrong?"

Silence filled the room again until it was broken by the reading of the verdict.

"Guilty!!!"

He closes the book and you are escorted out of the room. You have no idea where you are going, but your gut tells you that it is not good.

When Did You First Learn About Hell?

I'm going to end the story there, because we all know where it is going and I can no longer stomach the descriptions.

The "you" in this story describes millions of people that have lived good lives, doing well unto others, but for whatever reason, they did not buy the story about the Creator and His Son and their need to believe in Him.

According to the CAM (Currently Accepted Message of mainstream Christianity), this person will be sentenced to an eternity of physical pain and mental torment based solely on the answer to a yes or no question.

"Did he/she accept Jesus as his/her Savior?"

I'm not for a second going to argue about this with God, because if that is the rule, then that is the rule.

What we are going to do is what we have done throughout this entire book. That is, we are challenging those who have assumed they are correct in identifying the rules and consequences, and simply see if their story is solid or if there is another explanation that makes much more sense.

The concept of Hell has become such a huge part of our daily life that it is hard for us to pinpoint the first time we were even taught about it.

Do you remember where you were when you were first introduced to this idea of Hell?

If I am remembering correctly, it is possible that Yosemite Sam was the first to paint the picture for me.

Do you remember the scene where the devil tells Sam that he will let him go if he can just somehow catch a certain "wascally wabbit"?

My point is that the concept of Hell is so intermingled into everyday things that we never stop to question the validity of it.

On top of that, people whom we have trusted have told us that it is definitely real.

Did you ever stop and wonder how they know?

I asked an old pastor friend of mine that question once and he told me that when God calls a man to become a minister, He reveals these deep mysteries to them.

How convenient.

The CAM teacher knows, because it's his/her job to know, and we are not supposed to question it, right?

Assuming for a moment that you find this to be as peculiar as I do, where do you think these teachers came up with the idea of Hell?

Was it the Bible that first introduced them to it?

I don't think so.

They heard about it the same way most people did, that is, from somebody they trusted.

Where did the person they trusted hear it from?

Sure, it can be argued that the concept is in the Bible, but my point is that most people believed in Hell before the thought to question it ever came into their minds.

At least that's how it went for me.

By the time I cracked my Bible for myself, I already "knew" that Hell existed and who all was probably going to be there in the end. Then, as I followed along while the preacher read the Good Book, I saw exactly the picture he was painting and it made sense.

Does "Hell" Make Sense?

Does the idea of "Hell" make sense to you?

According to most CAM teachers, Hell is a prison for sinners, and not just any prison, but actually one that is far worse than any prison camp that has ever existed.

Think about the scariest scene you have ever seen on television, and then multiply that by a billion!

Some descriptions that I have heard, from people that "know" a lot about the subject, have included details like, (of course), fire over your entire body, worms eating your flesh, smells of death and worse, severe mental anguish, and the sounds of screaming and pain in all directions.

When I stop and try to picture this "place", I feel physically ill.

Why would God create this place?

What is the purpose?

Is it for corrections?

It can't be because it is eternal!

Corrections are temporary and designed to "correct" a problem.

Is it for revenge on the sinners?

Does God hate it when people make bad decisions so much that He has to torture them forever?

Most CAM members will argue from the point that who burns in this prison is not up to God, but up to the individual who ends up there.

That is quite a convenient answer I think.

That argument reminds me of people who do not think consumers should have the right to sue tobacco companies when they end up with lung cancer.

They are the ones who made the decision to puff the cancer stick 20 times a day, right?

This argument takes ALL of the blame off of the creator of the problem. If cigarettes did not exist, then no one would die from them. The blame clearly lies with the creator of the drug.

So why does God not share in the blame when it comes to Hell?

He made us human and then expects us to change or else be thrown into a fiery pit forever and that is somehow our fault?

Why isn't this argument used for people who murder their

wives?

Clearly if she had not said the wrong thing, he wouldn't have had to shoot her, right?

I'm sure he warned her, so it is her fault!!!

Again, let me say that if this was God's way, then that is just how it has to be, but we are going to look into it a little bit and see if by chance somebody has been confused about God's plan.

Is God a Good Parent?

Are you a parent?

If you are, is there anything that your child could do wrong that would cause you to burn them?

Although I am certain that such psychotic parents have existed and probably still do exist, most of the world would agree that this sort of behavior is horrible.

The truth is that no matter how bad of a day you have with your child, you wouldn't go start a fire in the backyard with the sole intention of using it to correct your child.

So why then do some believe God is this type of parent?

Did God put such effort and design into His creation just to destroy some of us in a big fire?

The concept of Hell in not only false, but it couldn't be any more illogical.

A good parent makes decisions for his children.

They keep their kids from harm.

The truth is simple…

God, by definition, is Love.

Love could never burn someone just because that someone didn't return the love.

Yes, it is true that God is also just, but what the CAM has failed to see, is that justice was served when Jesus paid our penalties on the cross.

God is satisfied with the sacrifice of Jesus.

Why aren't we?

The World of the Dead

Hell is mentioned daily in cartoons, by television preachers, in comedies, in dramas, in suspense movies, but if it is real, where is the first place it should be mentioned?

This is where deductive reasoning plays a major role when trying to make sense of all of this.

That is to say that oftentimes it is good to look for what is missing from the picture in order to get a full understanding of what is actually going on.

So if God created a torture chamber, who should have been the first ones to be made aware of it?

How about the first people to ever be given the opportunity to disobey God's Law?

How about Adam and Eve?

Did God warn them of the consequences of their actions?

Genesis 2:16-17...

And the LORD God commanded the man, saying, "Of every tree of the garden you may freely eat; but of the tree of the knowledge of good and evil you shall not eat, for in the day that you eat of it you shall surely die."

What does that mean….to die?

H4191 מוּת mu^th *mooth*

A primitive root; to *die* (literally or figuratively); causatively to *kill:* - X at all, X crying, (be) dead (body, man, one), (put to, worthy of) death, destroy (-er), (cause to, be like to, must) die, kill, necro [-mancer], X must needs, slay, X surely, X very suddenly, X in [no] wise.

There it is plain and simple. It means to be dead, that is, NOT ALIVE!

What does the Bible say death is?

H4194 מָוֶת ma^veth *maw'-veth*

From H4191; *death* (natural or violent); concretely the *dead*, their place or state (*hades*); figuratively *pestilence*, *ruin:* - (be) dead ([-ly]), death, die (-d).

Death is then by definition the place or state of the being after the body dies.

So God told Adam and Eve that the consequence of their disobedience to His one law was to die and to remain dead.

The worst punishment they faced was to not exist!

By contrast to the torture chamber we were taught about that doesn't seem so bad, but think about this for a few minutes.

As a being that is alive can you imagine simply not being in existence?

I absolutely love life in the good times and in the bad.

I cannot imagine not having the gift, the chance, and the freedom to live life to its fullest.

I'm sure it was the same for Adam and Eve. The thought of not existing must have been just as horrifying for them as it is for me. They didn't have children yet, but I do and when I think about not existing and never seeing them again it makes me sick.

I hold on to the hope that we will all be together on the other side, but if that wasn't the case I would be the most miserable man on the planet.

What happens to the meaning of this life if there is no afterlife?

This life would have no meaning whatsoever, save live for pleasure until you die because at that point it doesn't even matter!

However, we believe this is not the case. Our bodies will die but our true life, our spirit, moves on to exists in eternity.

Back to the point at hand, I'm am sure Adam and Eve would have thought about their choice a little bit more had they been aware of the place of torment you and I were taught about. Maybe they would have still messed up, or perhaps that would have been the design of the creator still the same, but to let your creation be aware of the consequences of their actions AHEAD OF TIME seems like a very fair and kind principle to follow.

As it is, they *were* told ahead of time what it was they would face if they made the wrong choice. They in fact made the wrong choice as we all know and we believe that to have been by design as well as we will discuss in chapter seven.

The fact of the matter is that God didn't mention a place of eternal torture to Adam and Eve.

He didn't mention it to Abraham or Isaac or Jacob.

He failed to mention it to Moses and the rest of the crew that came out of Egypt.

He didn't mention it to the prophets, not to the wise Solomon, not to Samuel, nor anyone else in the entire Old Testament.

<u>The concept for a place of eternal torture and punishment does not exist in the Old Testament anywhere!</u>

The King James Bible contains the word "hell" thirty one times in the Old Testament.

Wait a second though.

The word "hell" is an English word.

What is the *real* word used in the Hebrew that was translated "hell" by King James and the crew?

It is "shehole".

H7585 שְׁאוֹל שְׁאֹל sh^{e}'o^l sh^{e}'o^l *sheh-ole', sheh-ole'*

From H7592; *hades* or the world of the dead (as if a subterranean *retreat*), including its accessories and inmates: - grave, hell, pit.

So by definition shehole is simply the place where the dead are stored. It is the world of the dead. It is translated in the KJV Bible as the grave, hell, or pit. It is translated "hell" 31 times, but "shehole" is mentioned sixty five times. The other times it is translated as grave or pit.

Doesn't that seem just a little funny to you?

It does to me.

They had one word with one meaning yet it gets three different words in the English which, to us, have very different meanings.

Here is an extremely great example of how the meanings of things get changed when the meanings themselves are tampered with.

When you see "hell", you think of the torture chamber.

When you see "grave" you think of the cemetery.

When you see "pit" you think of a hole in the ground.

These describe three very different places in the English language, but it becomes completely clear what this place is when the original meaning it found out and applied.

When someone died, before the events at the cross, they went into a dormant state and were kept in "shehole", or the world of the dead, until their resurrection.

When I talk to pastors/preachers/teachers I ask them where

hell is in the Old Testament and most of them agree that it doesn't exist there.

So naturally the next question I ask is, "So when does it get mentioned?"

This part truly makes me laugh out loud (LOL for those of us who can't read full text).

Their answer is that it doesn't get mentioned until Jesus mentions it I the gospels!

First things first, what does the word "gospel" mean?

It means the "good news".

So really the good news should have started like this...

"and Jesus said to His disciples, 'Boys, I've got really good news and some really baaaaddddd news. Which do you want first?'"

I mean, before the good news, the bad news was that without a Savior we would cease to exist, but, as a divine surprise, God kept this secret hidden from the beginning of time to unleash on mankind the supposed truth of an everlasting torture chamber where humans would really go if they indeed chose incorrectly as Adam did!

Does this humor you as much as it does me?

Are they serious about this?!

So the savior of the world comes and really only reveals that things are so much worse than we could ever have expected or imagined.

After all, mankind had been left in the dark since the

beginning of time. I'm sure upon the announcement of such a place Adam and Eve and everyone else would have gasped and been really upset with God (of course they couldn't because they were, you know, dead!).

Let's get completely serious again and look at what Jesus was really talking about when He walked the earth 2000 years ago.

In the New Testament, you will find that Jesus used two different words that King James and the gang translated into "hell".

These two Greek words are "gehenna", and "hades".

You should notice that the second word looks familiar because it is in the definition of the first word we looked at, "shehole".

One of the first places "hades" is found in the New Testament is… KJV… ***Matthew 16:18…***

And I say also unto thee, That thou art Peter, and upon this rock I will build my church; and the gates of hell shall not prevail against it.

G86 ᾅδης hadēs *hah'-dace*
From G1 (as a negative particle) and G1492; properly *unseen*, that is, "Hades" or the place (state) of departed souls: - grave, hell.

It appears that this place is the same place mentioned in the Old Testament. In fact, as we just pointed out the word "hades" is actually in the definition of the word "shehole". They are both the place of departed souls, and the world of the dead.

If you study this out, you will find that every human went to “shehole/hades” when they died.

It was not just for “bad” people.

It was basically a symbolic holding cell.

Think about it. If God had two destinations to choose from, how would He know where to put a person unless He first judged them?

There is only 1 Day of Judgment described in the Bible to determine your final destination.

“Shehole/Hades” was just the place to keep the dead until that hour we least expected came.

The City Dump

The other Greek word that Jesus used that was translated “hell” was “gehenna”.

Most CAM teachers will not let this one go without a fight, but let’s take a look at it and you can decide for yourself what it means.

It was the first word Jesus uses in the New Testament that was translated into “hell”… ***Matthew 5:22...***

But I say to you that whoever is angry with his brother without a cause shall be in danger of the judgment. And whoever says to his brother, 'Raca!' shall be in danger of the council. But whoever says, 'You fool!' shall be in danger of hell fire.

G1067 γέεννα geenna *gheh'-en-nah*
Of Hebrew origin ([H1516] and [H2011]); *valley of* (the son of)

Hinnom; *gehenna* (or *Ge-Hinnom*), a valley of Jerusalem, used (figuratively) as a name for the place (or state) of everlasting punishment: - hell.

When we discuss this word with CAM leaders, they usually start by pointing to the last part of the definition here "used (figuratively) as a name for the place (or state) of everlasting punishment". We are going to look at this in just a bit, but before we do, let's look at "the valley of Hinnom". This physical place is first found in ***Jeremiah 7:30-31...***

For the children of Judah have done evil in My sight," says the LORD. "They have set their abominations in the house which is called by My name, to pollute it. And they have built the high places of Tophet, which is in the Valley of the Son of Hinnom, to burn their sons and their daughters in the fire, which I did not command, nor did it come into My heart.

"The Valley of the son of Hinnom" is where they were burning their own children as a sacrifice to the false god Molech. Notice how God says "***which I did not command, nor did it come into My heart.***" He called it an abomination to burn their children in the fire!

What would you call it?

Be prepared to answer that question in a few moments.

By definition the word "gehenna" means the valley of the son of Hinnom, but whoever wrote the definition of the word says it also is "used (figuratively) as a name for the place (or state) of everlasting punishment", and of course the word "hell" is the only word that King James and his posse translated the word into.

I have a few problems with this based on nothing less than

precise and sensible logic.

Problem number one is, why in the world would King James translate two very different words into the same word "hell"? How could he possibly find it logical to call "hades" AND "ghenna" all by the same word? They do not mean the same things and they certainly do not mean what "hell" was thought to be then or now by most unstudied people.

Perhaps King James and the gang were already influenced into believing that "hell", the place of eternal punishment and torture, existed or perhaps they wanted to be a key part in making millions more believe that it existed by using that word.

After all, religion generally, and particularly the belief in "hell", can influence people into being controlled by the ones who are offering the answer or the escape from such a place.

So again, the first problem we have is either based on ignorance or straight up manipulation, two things that do not really need to be found in a group trying to translate and communicate the Bible to anyone else on the planet.

Secondly, who gets to say that this place is used figuratively of a place of eternal punishment?

The concept didn't exist before and was certainly not explained, implied, or brought to light in any manner by Christ.

We would have to know that this was what Christ meant when He was using this word, and there is absolutely no way that we could possibly know that now.

Wait a second… actually we can.

Here is the case where deductive reasoning comes in handy.

What is there?

The word “ghenna”, which everyone back then knew to be the valley of the son of Hinnom or the burning trash heap on the outskirts of town, is “there”.

What is not there?

Jesus explaining that He was using this word figuratively of a different place is **not** “there”, and apparently the place He was supposed to be comparing it to has no name of its own!

“Ghenna” is the valley of the son of Hinnom, but how does this line of speculation get into a dictionary?

There is simply no basis for assuming that to be true. This part of the definition may be true in the sense that people today use this word figuratively of an eternal torture chamber, but how do the writers of the dictionary sleep at night by saying that this is how Christ was using the word?

Simple logic shows that there is no basis whatsoever for assuming Christ meant anything else but what the word actually meant to the people of those days.

The third issue needs some pretext.

I entered into a discussion with a much studied CAM member who is very well respected in his church. He reminded me of what most of my previous Bible teachers taught. When studying the scripture one has to consider who is talking, who they are talking to, the culture of the time so as to understand figures of speech and whatnot, and the pre-existing knowledge of the group the person was talking to is so as to understand more how the receivers of the message would understand and interpret the message given to them. This respected CAM member and teacher reminded me of this as we entered into our discussion so that I would not take things out of context or presume things to be there that are not. Ironically, he was the very one who did not follow his own logic. Please allow me to explain.

The Case of the Missing Word

Jesus is speaking to people in Israel 2000 years ago and he says this in ***Matthew 5:29...***

If your right eye causes you to sin, pluck it out and cast it from you; for it is more profitable for you that one of your members perish, than for your whole body to be cast into hell.

The original word that King James translated into "hell" here is "Ghenna".

So think about this.

Let's say that I am a Jew living 2,000 years ago and I have no prior knowledge or even the concept of a place of everlasting punishment in my thoughts.

Jesus just tells me that it is better for one member to perish than to be thrown into "ghenna".

Immediately I think of the place He just mentioned to me. I look over my right shoulder and low and behold there it is, the valley of the son of Hinnom. I can smell the smoke coming from it. I know that this place is where the city trash is taken to and is burned. I also know that if you are a hard core criminal you could end up facing the most dreaded punishment of not only the death penalty but after you are dead your body being thrown into this fire pit.

Then the CAM comes along and makes it just so confusing for this poor guy because they say that Jesus was simply using the word "gehenna" as the closest comparison to the place of eternal torture that they later invented.

The problem is that no one ever informed him of this news until hundreds of years later, *after* he was dead.

This poor guy thinks Jesus is talking about the real "gehenna" and not this new place that was kept secret for so long.

It just seems to me that Jesus, being the creator of all things including us, would actually be able to communicate with us effectively.

Doesn't that make sense?

Not according to the CAM.

They say Jesus was using "gehenna" to explain what THAT place, the "real hell", was actually like.

Here is the crux of my point.

WHERE is the REAL WORD for that place?

What is the place of eternal torture really called?

Why was it kept secret only to be revealed during the "good news" period and then not given a name of its own?

This is what we call the "**Case of the Missing Word**".

Wouldn't it be fair for Jesus to have said…?

"Hey guys, there's a place in the afterlife that is a place of

eternal punishment. If you do not believe in me and ask for forgiveness of your sins and try to live a good life then you will go there and burn in a fire forever and ever. You will be in torment day and night, you will beg for mercy and receive none, you will cry out to God and He will only make the fire hotter and watch you twist and writhe in pain and suffering of the like in which you have never even imagined before….etc. etc. etc. and the only place you have here to compare it to is gehenna, so while I am here I am going to call it gehenna because I haven't quite chosen a name for the real place yet."

I guess I couldn't blame Him for the whole name thing, after all what could you call that place in one word to accurately get your message across?

"Hell" I suppose would work, but Jesus never used the word "hell". He used the word "gehenna" and never said anything to indicate that He was comparing it to another place. "Gehenna" was a real place. The people Jesus was speaking to knew all about it. Jesus did not have to explain it to them because they were all very familiar with the city dump.

Do you know what they were not familiar with?

They were not familiar with a place where God burns people forever. They had never heard of this place, nor did Jesus ever mention such a place.

The only other place "hell" shows up is in ***2Peter 2:4...***

For if God did not spare the angels who sinned, but cast them down to hell and delivered them into chains of darkness, to be reserved for judgment;

The word for "hell" here is "tartaros"

G5020ταρταρόω tartaroō *tar-tar-o'-o* From Τάρταρος Tartaros (the deepest *abyss* of Hades); to *incarcerate* in eternal torment: -

cast down to hell.

Once again, uh oh right? The definition includes the words "eternal torment". Let's think about this a minute. "Tartaros" is literally the deepest abyss of Hades, which we know is simply the world of the dead. The punishment of being in Hades or the sentence being served there is death, which is the opposite of being alive and conscious, not eternal burning flames of torment. "Tartaros" is simply the deepest part of that place, signifying the severity of the act those did to deserve to be there.

Regardless, this place called hades or shehole gets destroyed by Christ Himself in the "lake of fire" as found in the book of Revelation. So the angels trapped there couldn't be tortured there for forever, because this place gets done away with. Even better yet, look at the verse again. The angels were cast there UNTIL the judgment!

So they were in a place of eternal punishment UNTIL?

Can you see how that doesn't work?

You cannot be tortured forever if you are only kept there until a certain point. This is the only place this word is used in the entire Bible and the context in which it is used proves that the part of its definition that suggests eternity is nothing more than a conjecture based on the belief of the ones who made the dictionary.

The Lake of Fire

When I debate/discuss our beliefs with CAM leaders it is easy to get them to admit that "Shehole"/"Hades", "Gehenna" and "Tartaros" are not the place they are really referring to when they talk about the place of eternal punishment they call "hell".

Before our discussion they would have preached hell, and probably out of those scriptures and more like them, but after our talks they could only do so with a seared conscious because it is easy to see that their hell cannot be found in the words of Christ. Once we get this out of the way, the only thing left to talk about is the Lake of Fire first found in ***Revelations 19:20...***

Then the beast was captured, and with him the false prophet who worked signs in his presence, by which he deceived those who received the mark of the beast and those who worshiped his image. These two were cast alive into the lake of fire burning with brimstone.

In chapter four we explained and demonstrated how everything in the entire book of Revelation was in signs. Remember that John was seeing symbolic visions and writing down what he saw. Some of these symbols are explained by John, like that the candle sticks represented the churches and the stars represented angels.

Most of the symbols are not explained.

We took the time to give you our explanation of the symbolism used in chapter 21 regarding the New Heaven and Earth and the New Jerusalem. So now we will take a look at the lake fire and what it is symbolic of. We will examine its purpose and ultimately see that it is something that should be embraced by mankind, and not feared as we were taught. ***Revelations 20:14-15...***

Then Death and Hades were cast into the lake of fire. This is the second death. And anyone not found written in the Book of Life was cast into the lake of fire.

Death and Hades were cast into the lake of fire which is the second death.

First thing first, is death a living being?

No, it is not.

It is the state of a living being when the body dies before it has been resurrected by Christ.

Is Hades a living being?

No, it is not.

It is a place, physical or not, that is the world of the dead.

So if Hades is/was a physical place, then it perhaps could be literally burned up, but what about death?

Death is the state of the being. Can a "state", a condition, or an idea be literally burned up in a real fire?

Of course it cannot.

This gives us an immediate clue as to the true nature and purpose for this fire. Now let's look at ***Revelations 21:8...***

But the cowardly, unbelieving, abominable, murderers, sexually immoral, sorcerers, idolaters, and all liars shall have their part in the lake which burns with fire and brimstone, which is the second death."

Here John says that all these bad people "***shall have their part in the lake".*** This is the part that we are most excited to explain in this chapter.

Fire Symbolism

Before we explain what the Lake is symbolic of, let's look at other places fire shows up in the New Testament and see what it is being symbolically used for. Check out ***Matthew 3:10-12...***

And even now the ax is laid to the root of the trees. Therefore every tree which does not bear good fruit is cut down and thrown into the fire. I indeed baptize you with water unto repentance, but He who is coming after me is mightier than I, whose sandals I am not worthy to carry. He will baptize you with the Holy Spirit and fire. His winnowing fan is in His hand, and He will thoroughly clean out His threshing floor, and gather His wheat into the barn; but He will burn up the chaff with unquenchable fire."

Here, John the Baptist tells the people that Jesus is coming to take care of business. When he says "***And even now the ax is laid to the root of the trees***", does it appear that John thinks the time is close or far off?

Obviously he thinks it is close. He knew that Jesus was here to wrap some things up, yet even today, 2,000 years later, we are being warned that the time has finally come.

So who is right?

Was Jesus coming to take care of some things, or was He just going to start some things?

John said that He was going to baptize them with fire. Baptisms usually take place in bodies of water such as rivers, streams, and oh yeah… lakes!

He also says that Jesus is going to do some separating. He is going to separate the wheat from the chaff and burn up the chaff.

It doesn't sound like the crop has much choice in the matter, does it?

It is clear that all of this that was described was all about to happen right then, 2,000 years ago. As we have just explained in previous chapters and will continue to explain, this is obviously talking about the Day of Judgment and again it is spoken of as an event that was at hand or just about to happen. As we keep moving forward you will see that this is certainly the case.

Let's examine the explanation of the parable of the wheat and the tears Jesus gives to the people… Matthew 13:37-43...

He answered and said to them: "He who sows the good seed is the Son of Man. The field is the world, the good seeds are the sons of the kingdom, but the tares are the sons of the wicked one. The enemy who sowed them is the devil, the harvest is the end of the age, and the reapers are the angels. Therefore as the tares are gathered and burned in the fire, so it will be at the end of this age. The Son of Man will send out His angels, and they will gather out of His kingdom all things that offend, and those who practice lawlessness, and will cast them into the furnace of fire. There will be wailing and gnashing of teeth. Then the righteous will shine forth as the sun in the kingdom of their Father. He who has ears to hear, let him hear!

When Jesus says "He who has ears to hear, let him hear!" He means that there is more to understand than what is on the surface.

Once again, it is a mystery that must be looked into in order to understand its true meaning.

So the harvest is at the end of the world. Also take note that this sounds a whole lot like the judgment of the world that John the Baptist spoke of as an event that was about to happen, which signifies the end of the world and, by implication, the beginning of a new one.

Another pattern we find here that is repeated is this separation of the good from the bad, the wheat from the tears, the fruit bearing trees and the bad trees, the sheep and the goats, etc. We will keep seeing this pattern as we move on. This passage also gives us a clue to the nature of the fire Jesus is speaking about. When the wheat and tears are gathered up, the tears are burned and when they burn they simply burn up and are destroyed. Another way to look at this is that He is simply purifying his harvest. Look at verses ***49-50...***

So shall it be at the end of the world: the angels shall come forth, and sever the wicked from among the just, And shall cast them into the furnace of fire: there shall be wailing and gnashing of teeth.

Again we see the division that is to come at the time of judgment or at the end of the age, which is of course the harvest and although it sounds scary, it is symbolic and will all make sense when we get to the end of this section. ***Luke 12:49-51...***

I am come to send fire on the earth; and what will I, if it be already kindled? But I have a baptism to be baptized with; and how am I straitened till it be accomplished! Suppose ye that I am come to give peace on earth? I tell you, Nay; but rather division:

Once again Jesus says He came to bring fire and division on the earth.

It sounds like He meant right then or shortly after He makes these statements.

Could this be the same fire of judgment that He keeps referring to?

He keeps talking about fire, judgment, division of the good from the bad, and the end of the world and He does so as if the end is near right at the that time, 2,000 years ago.

The Accuser

The CAM says that Judgment Day is coming, but when does Jesus say it will be? ***John 12:23-33...***

But Jesus answered them, saying, "The hour has come that the Son of Man should be glorified. Most assuredly, I say to you, unless a grain of wheat falls into the ground and dies, it remains alone; but if it dies, it produces much grain. He who loves his life will lose it, and he who hates his life in this world will keep it for eternal life. If anyone serves Me, let him follow Me; and where I am, there My servant will be also. If anyone serves Me, him My Father will honor. "Now My soul is troubled, and what shall I say? 'Father, save Me from this hour'? But for this purpose I came to this hour. Father, glorify Your name." Then a voice came from heaven, saying, "I have both glorified it and will glorify it again." Therefore the people who stood by and heard it said that it had thundered. Others said, "An angel has spoken to Him." Jesus answered and said, "This voice did not come because of Me, but for your sake. Now is the judgment of this world; now the ruler of this world will be cast out. And I, if I am lifted up from the earth, will draw all peoples to Myself." This He said, signifying by what death He would die.

How much more obvious can it get?

He says the hour is come that He is to be glorified, which implies that it is the hour that He becomes victorious.

If the grain of wheat dies, it produces much grain. He was talking about Himself dying and bringing forth fruit through His death.

Finally He announces that the judgment of the world was "Now", or "then" to us in the present, and that the prince of this world would be cast out. This is, again, exactly what we find in Revelation, or the disclosure of Christ. ***Revelations 12:9-12...***

So the great dragon was cast out, that serpent of old, called the Devil and Satan, who deceives the whole world; he was cast to the earth, and his angels were cast out with him. Then I heard a loud voice saying in heaven, "Now salvation, and strength, and the kingdom of our God, and the power of His Christ have come, for the accuser of our brethren, who accused them before our God day and night, has been cast down. And they overcame him by the blood of the Lamb and by the word of their testimony, and they did not love their lives to the death. Therefore rejoice, O heavens, and you who dwell in them! Woe to the inhabitants of the earth and the sea! For the devil has come down to you, having great wrath, because he knows that he has a short time."

We were taught that this is a future event, but Jesus himself says it was happening right then.

Here we see the Devil cast down on the earth, and we also see that his time was short.

We see that "now" salvation and the kingdom is here.

Jesus said that the kingdom was at hand so many times while He walked the earth and we can now easily see that this passage in Revelation is talking about the same time period.

Also, notice that the Devil is called "***the accuser of our brethren***" when it says he was cast down. In chapter 4, we showed you that the end of the world was symbolic of the end of the Law.

Think about this for a moment…

If the Devil was going to accuse you of something to God, what would he accuse you of???

Obviously the Law was the written rules of God and therefore breaking the Law was the only thing that fits. If the Law ended with the death of Jesus, then what does the accuser have on you?

The Law is over; therefore the accuser is cast down!

The Separation

Jesus said He came to bring fire and to bring division.

Who or what was going to be burned?

Who would escape this judgment and who wouldn't?

In chapter 2, we explained that when Jesus died on the cross, He represented ALL of creation. Remember this passage we discussed… ***John 8:21-24...***

> ***Then Jesus said to them again, "I am going away, and you will seek Me, and will die in your sin.***

Where I go you cannot come." So the Jews said, "Will He kill Himself, because He says, 'Where I go you cannot come'?" And He said to them, "You are from beneath; I am from above. You are of this world; I am not of this world. Therefore I said to you that you will die in your sins; for if you do not believe that I am He, you will die in your sins."

We covered the fact that no one believed on Him in chapter 2. Not even His disciples believed just as Jesus told them right before He went to the cross. ***John 16:30-32...***

Now we are sure that You know all things, and have no need that anyone should question You. By this we believe that You came forth from God." Jesus answered them, "Do you now believe? Indeed the hour is coming, yes, has now come, that you will be scattered, each to his own, and will leave Me alone. And yet I am not alone, because the Father is with Me.

So no one believed, and those who do not believe will have to stay here and die in their sins. So the judgment is coming, and the glorifying of Christ, and when Jesus dies and leaves no one can follow Him, but they must remain here and die in their sins.

What is this death He is talking about?

We'll get to that in just a minute, but first let's look at the division Christ talks about as we wrap up this story. ***Matthew 25:31-34, 41...***

"<u>When the Son of Man comes in His glory</u>, and all the holy angels with Him, then He will sit on the throne of His glory. All the nations will be gathered before Him, and He will separate them one from another, as a shepherd divides his sheep from the goats.

And He will set the sheep on His right hand, but the goats on the left. Then the King will say to those on His right hand, 'Come, you blessed of My Father, inherit the kingdom prepared for you from the foundation of the world:

"Then He will also say to those on the left hand, 'Depart from Me, you cursed, into the everlasting fire prepared for the devil and his angels:

Again, please notice that this happens when Christ comes in His glory. He will separate the sheep from the goats, just like the wheat and the tears, the good and the bad and He will burn up the bad side and grant eternal life to the good side.

This is the same division He said that He has brought with Him along with the fire that would burn it all up.

As we have continued to demonstrate, these events were all part of the judgment of the world, which we have shown is the day of the cross.

So if all of this happened on the day of the cross, then who was it that burned up in the fires of judgment?

Who was tossed into the everlasting fires to be destroyed?

Who are the people from the following passage? ***Rev 21:8...***

But the cowardly, unbelieving, abominable, murderers, sexually immoral, sorcerers, idolaters, and all liars shall have their part in the lake which burns with fire and brimstone, which is the second death."

Look at what Paul says here in ***2Corinthians 5:14...***

For the love of Christ compels us, because we

judge thus: that if One died for all, then all died;

It is so very simple.

When Jesus died, nobody believed.

When Jesus died, ALL died.

Obviously physical death did not happen for ALL people.

What type of death took place when ALL died?

Symbolically we ALL died because Jesus death was symbolic of the End of the World.

His resurrection was symbolic of the beginning of the New World.

The Lake of Fire is simply the symbolism used in the vision that John sees and it is symbolic of forgiveness!!!

Why would such a scary symbol be used for forgiveness?

Think about the major significance of the act. Jesus death symbolized the death of us ALL.

The Sins of the Whole World were placed on Him!!!

What do you think that felt like? Do you think it felt good?

The Lake of Fire is symbolic of the torturous death that Jesus suffered that resulted in the forgiveness of the World.

When Jesus died, the sin that separated us from God was removed from our account. This was foreseen by the writers of the Old Covenant… Look here in ***Psalms 103:12...***

As far as the east is from the west, So far has He removed our transgressions from us.

The separation of the good and the bad, the wheat and the chaff, the sheep and the goats, are all symbolic of the separation of us from our transgressions.

<u>Your sins were separated from you and burned up in the Lake of Fire, along with the Devil and Death and Hades!!! Jesus death was the End of Sin!!!</u>

Think about it…

How does forgiveness work?

We ALL have had friends betray us in one way or another haven't we?

Most of us probably are still friends with people who have hurt us in the past.

In order to forgive someone, you have to separate the person from the deeds they did that hurt you. If you cannot look at them without constantly remembering what they did, then it will make you miserable every time you are around them.

<u>He is Satisfied</u>

When Jesus died for our sins, God took out His anger and wrath on Him. He took our evil deeds and placed them on Christ and Jesus endured the pain for us. The final result of the righteous act of Jesus is the separation of our evil deeds from us in God's eyes.

You see, God made this place. He made us ALL. Why would He make us and then burn some of us? That doesn't make any sense.

The CAM often argues that people who do not believe in Jesus do not deserve to be forgiven.

Does anyone deserve forgiveness?

Some might, some might not, but that isn't even the point of the entire thing.

God forgave us because it was what He wanted to do!!!

In ALL my years in the CAM world, I never once heard anyone talk about the benefit that God got out of this forgiveness. We were always so concerned about whether or not we got to go to heaven that we failed to see that this plan was beneficial to our Creator as well. ***Isaiah 43:25...***

> ***I, even I, am He who blots out your transgressions <u>for My own sake</u>; And I will not remember your sins.***

<u>He did it for Himself too!!!</u>

Forgiving you felt good to Him!!!

His anger was satisfied!!! ***Isaiah 53:11...***

> ***He shall see the labor of His soul, and be satisfied. By His knowledge My righteous Servant shall justify many, For He shall bear their iniquities.***

<u>When Hell Freezes Over</u>

Pigs may never fly, but think of ALL the cool things that will happen when Hell freezes over.

Hopefully this book will help begin the cooling process.

The fact of the matter is and always will be that the concept of an eternal place of burning punishment simply does not exist in the Bible. It is a contrived story used by the people who made it up to control the people that sat under their teachings. Over a long period of time the concept became integrated into peoples thinking and they started believing it, as many people still do to this day.

Most CAM members and leaders are well intentioned. We cannot blame them for spreading the beliefs of Hell. As we did for so long, they simply believe what they were told without question.

When you grow up hearing about this horrible place and then you see descriptions of fire and other horrors in the Bible, it is hard not to believe Hell is real.

As a matter of fact, coming to the conclusion that Hell is merely a nightmare and not real was not easy for us. It took a lot of studying as well as a lot of intense emotional soul searching. It was one of the most difficult, yet most rewarding things we have ever experienced.

If you are not yet convinced, we don't blame you. All we ask is that you consider the possibilities and look into it. You won't regret it.

Jumping Through Hoops of Fire!!!

When you know that you have betrayed a friend, it becomes very difficult to look them in the eyes. It is especially torturous when that person becomes aware of what you have done and is not in the forgiving mood. There is almost always a separation that happens between the two of you as a brick wall is built in your heads.

Sometimes that wall stays built forever and the friendship is never reconciled.

Sometimes it takes years for the wall to come down as you jump through hoops, hoping to prove to your friend that you are sorry and hope that the trust can be rebuilt.

Sometimes, though it is rare, the wall comes down quickly. This is only possible when the one who has been wronged is strong enough to forgive you.

You, the one who is yearning for forgiveness, never have the power to tear down the wall.

You may wish the wall was gone, but the choice isn't yours.

Since the day Adam tasted the fruit from the tree of the knowledge of good and evil, mankind has been separated from God.

In an effort to tear down the wall that separated us from Him, Moses was given a list of hoops to jump through.

Although many have tried, (and continue to try), none have met the requirements of the Law. All have failed in their attempt to jump through the hoops.

2,000 years ago, God sent His Son, Jesus to our planet to see what He could do.

Before His final act, Jesus set the hoops on fire, hoping to make it very clear to ALL that this was an impossible task.

Do not try this at home!!!

Then, just as the spotlights were focusing on Him and everyone was ready to see what He was going to do to end the show, something unexpected happened.

The hoops exploded.

Then the lights went out.

Everything seemed to have gone wrong.

When the smoke finally cleared, they found Jesus, dead.

Sad and confused, they buried Him in a tomb.

This was supposed to be their Hope?

Jesus final act appeared to be a failed attempt.

Death on a cross is not a typical sign of victory.

But this day was different.

Jesus didn't jump through the hoops as many watched for Him to do.

Jesus took the hoops down.

God did what only He had the power to do.

At our weakest moment, when it was clear that we had no hope, God chose to forgive us.

We gave Him no reason to trust us.

We showed Him no indication that we were going to change.

If He was like any one of us, the wall would have never come down.

The Good News, however, is that God is not like us.

He did tear the wall down.

He forgave us ALL for no good reason.

He did the unexpected and He did it in the Hour We Least Expected!!!

The Hour We Least Expected

Chapter 7

The Gospel According To Us

Perhaps there is no better way to fully explain in a nutshell what it is that we believe than by telling our version of the main scope of the story of our history.

Destined to Fail

I recall the scene in the movie "The Matrix: Revolutions" when Agent Smith is speaking with the all-powerful and all seeing "Oracle" right before he takes her powers away from her. She had placed a plate of cookies on the table where she sat awaiting his entrance, because she, of course, knew he was coming. When he entered the room, he began his speech to her. During his speech he threw the plate of cookies against the wall and then reasoned out loud about whether or not she knew he was going to throw the cookies, and if she did then she purposely placed them there just for that moment.

He was struggling with the implications of her powers.

Did he and others do what she wanted them to do? Did she control them? Did they have free will?

Perhaps she only knew what they were going to do before they did it but didn't actually control them, but does her knowing everything in advance take the free will out of the equation?

Agent Smith couldn't understand the "why" of the thing he was dealing with. He knew what she could do, but "why" could she, and what other implications did this have?

We believe that God planned everything.

He chose us in Christ before the foundations of the world. He planned good works for us to do before we were born. He wrote history in advance and laid it all out for a bigger reason and bigger purpose.

We believe that God planned everything for many reasons, but one BIG reason for sure and that is to prove to us His unconditional love for us.

He placed Adam and Eve next to the tree on purpose and sent the serpent on purpose to tempt them, knowing that they would give in.

He set it all up ahead of time, making us destined to fail and fall flat on our faces so that we could know exactly what was pure and evil, good and bad, right from wrong, pleasure and discomfort, tension and release, tiredness and rest… etc.

He wanted us to know pain and suffering so as to be able to appreciate the coming perfection and pleasure. He wanted us to be in a mess that we ourselves could not get out of and He arranged for that to happen.

He made us weak to temptation. The fact that we are tempted at all implies that we have weaknesses.

He made us imperfect in order to show us perfect love because perfect love loves no matter what!

Perfect love says "I don't care what that person does to me, I will never stop loving them or showing my love for them."

Perfect love HOLDS NO RECORD OF WRONGS!

He is able to show this kind of love ONLY because we fell into a state far from perfection.

Anyone can love someone who is perfect. Anyone can love someone who loves them back. But God proves who He is, the All-Powerful, All-Knowing, God who created the Universe, by doing what others cannot.

While we were yet sinners, God showed His perfect love to us by sending His Son to die for us, and if this was the only way to show us perfect love then He planned for man to be imperfect from the start.

How could we know real love without real hate, or the best without the worst to compare it against!?

We could not!

So He gave us the gift of pain and suffering, toil and hard work then the rest and rewards from it all.

Why do we have the desire to work and build and make something in this world?

It is our nature given to us by our creator to teach us that nothing good is free.

How about the ultimate good? Was it free?

NO of course not, it costs a lot.

It didn't cost us a lot, rather it cost Him a lot.

It didn't cost money or simply force God to work something by His power and might, but rather cost so much more.

His own pain and suffering was the price He paid for you and me.

He created us destined to fail so that in the end He could express His perfect love for you and me by designing the solution to our mess to be something that would cause Him great pain and heartache.

How Do We Know God Loves Us?

A child doesn't know his dad loves him because his dad buys him whatever he wants, or buys his kids way onto a sports team or into a special club.

The child KNOWS his dad loves him when his dad makes sacrifices for him. The child knows his dad loves him when he attends every single ball game, chess match, music recital, swim meet, or whatever he is into, even when he could be doing something else with his time. It is when the dad didn't buy himself the new fishing rod or musical instruments or new body building machine, but instead gave those things up to pay for a better education for his son.

It is the sacrifice that proves the love.

How about in a marriage?

The honeymoon period is the easy part for a number of obvious reasons. Everything is fresh and new and the initial excitement of the new life can carry things for a while, but then one day the wills of two individuals, that developed separately over a period of 18+ years with the guidance of two very different families, start to collide in the realm of opinions over money, time, priorities and more.

That is when love will be tested!

That is when true love will either be present and show its face or something less than true love will show itself and feelings of resentment and guilt and so many others will come out and destroy the marriage.

When true love is present, so is sacrifice, dedication, honor, and loyalty.

It is then and only then, and never before, that the spouses can KNOW that they are truly loved by the other person.

God proves His love to us in that while we were still sinners He died for us and paid the ultimate price for us.

He did it for ALL of us and, no matter what happens from here on out, NOTHING can separate ANY OF US from God's perfect and true love!

It is impossible for someone to be led astray because God's love for that person is farther reaching than any distance the person seemingly strays from God.

Not one person on this planet can escape His love!

It is too late for them!

He already accomplished the work!

IT IS FINISHED!

He cannot and will not take it back now, nor would He want to.

Mankind was and is way past the initial creation period which I would equate to the honeymoon period. He knows of our shortcomings, our imperfections, and our dark desires. As a matter of fact, He Himself created us with those feelings in us and knew we would be the way that we are.

It is in spite of all of our flaws that He decided to reconcile us to Himself.

During a time of great despair, the likes of which had never been seen before or since, He poured out His wrath on Himself and took the pain and the suffering for us.

He executed judgment and grace at the same time.

That is the Judgment of the World that He was beginning to pour out and the Grace that was the shield of Himself that absorbed the judgment.

It was during this ultimate test of love and under the most horrific conditions that God displayed and proved His love for us.

This is how we can know that his love is real and everlasting.

The Purpose of the Law

He gave the Hebrew children the Law in order to shed some more light on their condition and thus make more vivid the contrast between what we were and what was considered to be perfect behavior.

Then Jesus came along and made that contrast so ridiculously vivid that there was no question in anyone's mind that we were all messed up, imperfect, and that there is nothing that we could do to fix it.

Jesus didn't always teach hope while He walked the earth. As a matter of fact He really stirred a lot of people up and only showed us more clearly our imperfections and the hopelessness we had in our ability to save ourselves through the fulfillment of the Law.

He was the Word in the flesh.

He was the Law and taught the Law to its fullest.

It wasn't until after the price was paid that He became the Prince of Peace.

God was still toiling with us until our debt was paid. Jesus said Himself that He came to bring fire and division, not peace. He was the Judge and was the Giver of Grace. He brought the Fire of Judgment and took it all upon Himself.

He seemed to double talk the entire time He was here because we did not understand that He was the Law and also was here to sacrifice Himself to kill the Law.

The Law or Word became flesh and then died.

When He was resurrected He came to us as the Prince of Peace and as the One who tore down the partition between us and God our Father.

His gracious side overtook or outweighed His judgmental side; therefore He died in judgment but rose in grace.

The Wrath and Judgment of God

As Jesus taught, the Judgment of the World was at hand

when He walked the earth 2,000 years ago.

On the Day of Judgment those without sin received eternal life and those with sin were punished.

The Day of Judgment, also referred to the Day of the Lord so many times in the Old Testament, was the day of the Cross.

Christ, being beaten and broken was carrying the sins of the entire world on Himself. He carried them up the hill, and then was lifted up on the cross on top of a mountain.

The sign of the Son of Man was in the sky that day, as He hung there with all eyes fixed on Him.

He bore all of mankind's sin on the Day of Judgment, and when the hammer fell, Christ was the only one who had sin and He was judged accordingly and the rest of us, who at that moment had no sin, were given eternal life.

We were changed in the twinkling of an eye and in an instant we were gathered up with Him.

When one died, that is Christ, we all died as it was foretold to the disciples that they (and in fact everyone) would remain here and die in their sins.

We were saved from God's wrath through Christ and now, since Jesus took the wrath for us, God is now satisfied and is not toiling with man's imperfections anymore.

Our sin was cancelled out by Christ, therefore that part of us died when He died and now that He rose again we are all living in Him whether we know it or not.

This was the great separation.

We are the sheep and the goats.

We are the two in the field and the two in the bed.

We are the ones who were thrown into the Lake of Fire and who dwell in the Kingdom of God.

The Lake of Fire burned up the bad in us and refined us so that only the good remained in God's eyes.

He did this to demonstrate His awesome abilities to be the God of Justice and the God who is by definition Love.

We were all spared from wrath and now we all live under His grace.

Death and Hades

Death and Hades were destroyed when Christ was resurrected.

No longer can anyone be in an unconscious state after their body dies because the condition of death, and death itself, in fact, has been destroyed.

The place where the dead were kept, Hades, no longer exists therefore cannot hold anyone in its cells.

This is the reason why Paul said that to be absent from the body is to be present with Christ. This could not be the case if death and Hades still existed.

Through Christ's victory over death, He destroyed it and released all the captives that death was holding. This was the Resurrection of the Dead. There are no longer any souls kept in reserve but ALL are now with Him, experiencing eternal life.

The Kingdom is Here

The parable of the treasure in the field and the pearls in the field is about us. This whole thing was never about how we could prove our love for Him, but rather how He proves His love for us. He loved us so much that He went and sold everything He had in order to come and pay for the field, which is all of creation, so that He would have the treasure held therein, which is us.

We are the pearls and we are the treasure.

He paid the price with His life and redeemed ALL of creation including the treasure that is we, His people, His children, His beloved.

Now the Kingdom, which is an invisible kingdom, is among us and only those who realize it can truly enjoy it in this lifetime.

Our job is to tell others the Good News and help them see the Kingdom around them so they too can live a life of freedom from guilt and shame, knowing that they are perfect in the sight of God.

What Now?

Now we help others to see the truth.

We start seeing other people as God sees them.

We treat other people as equals and as fellow brothers and sisters from the same Father.

We partake of the work of true ministry which is helping those who cannot help themselves.

We help the orphans, the widows, the children with cancer, the guy who needs help up to get back on his feet and begin life again.

We also take responsibility for ourselves and our own actions.

We start living a life that is full of respect for each other.

We start making this world a better place for ALL of mankind.

We all sacrifice ourselves to love and its work.

It is not a requirement to do so, but knowing the truth should be enough to compel most people to begin to develop a true love for life and their fellow man.

We celebrate humanity instead of judging our fellow imperfect humans.

The gospel provides a great framework of how to view ourselves and our world. It facilitates better self-driven responsibility. It allows us to celebrate our humanity and enjoy being who God made us to be. It gives us the ability to have compassion on other people in spite of our differences. It frees us from guilt and shame which frees us up to help others around us.

The gospel provides a better way for ALL of mankind and, once recognized, gives mankind the starting point in which it needs to function better as a society while still maintaining our personal freedoms and choices.

The Final Hour…

In Matthew 24, Jesus told His disciples that the End would

come like a thief in the night.

It would be sudden and would be at the time they least expected it.

The day He hung on the cross, bruised and beaten, torn, naked and bleeding, it appeared to all that He had lost.

This did not look like a moment of great victory.

It looked like the moment of the greatest defeat.

Who would have thought that the Glorification of the Son of Man would happen through His gruesome death?

Who would have thought that He had won any battle at that moment in time?

None did, and few have realized it in the past 2,000 years since the event.

The fact is, we have ALL come a long way since the events of the cross.

We used to see the world as a horrible place that is just getting worse.

If you will just take the time to reflect on the last couple centuries alone, you will see that this is not the case.

The world is getting better and the further along we get, the clearer the picture that He painted becomes.

Think about it… If a thief came to your house tonight, when would you realize it?

At what point would you know the whole story of how it all

happened?

It takes time to figure these things out and over the past 2,000 years, mankind has been getting closer and closer to the truth of what happened and how it happened.

Truth will not lie dormant forever. Just as in this case, it has made itself known, and it will continue to become clearer as time passes.

The end of the age and the beginning of the next came 2,000 years ago like a thief in the night.

It came in a way no one expected…

By the One no one expected…

In The Hour We Least Expected.

The Hour We Least Expected

We would like to hear from you.

For questions, comments, or for booking information, please visit our website at www.thehourweleastexpected.com.